D1369233

fIRST YEAR
WEEK BY WEEK

MAGGIE JONES

SMITHMARK

CONTENTS

weeks 27-39

6-9 months

weeks 40-52

9-12 months

Project editor
Charyn Jones

Project art editor
Christine Wood

Project assistant
Caroline Davison

Illustrators
Biz Hull
Shelagh McNicholas

Production
Mano Mylvaganam

Picture research
Abigail Ahern

This revised edition first published in 1993
by Conran Octopus Limited
37 Shelton Street
London WC2H 9HN

Text copyright © 1988 Maggie Jones
Artwork copyright © 1988 Conran Octopus

The right of Maggie Jones to be identified
as author of this work has been asserted
by her in accordance with the Copyright,
Designs and Patents Act 1988.

This edition first published in 1995 by
Smithmark Publishers, Inc.
16 East 32nd Street
New York, NY 10016

All rights reserved. No part of this
publication may be reproduced, stored in a
retrieval system or transmitted in any form
or by any means electronic, mechanical,
photocopying or otherwise, without first
obtaining written permission of the
copyright owner.

SMITHMARK books are available for bulk
purchase sales promotion and premium
use. For details write or call the manager of
special sales, SMITHMARK Publishers Inc.,
16 East 32nd Street, New York, NY 10016;
(212) 532–6600.

ISBN 0-8317-9421-6

Printed in Hong Kong

10 9 8 7 6 5 4 3 2 1

*i*NTRODUCTION

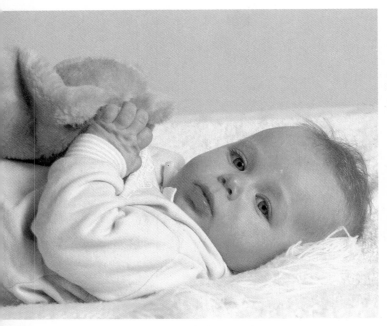

*t*his book is a week-by-week guide to the first year of your baby's life. It aims to describe in detail the various stages of a baby's progress, to give practical advice and to help parents cope with, and enjoy, their baby at every age.

Wherever possible, the information you will need appears on the page most appropriate to the age and stage your baby is at. However, this is not always feasible. First of all, the huge amount of information relevant to the early days has had to be spread over the first few weeks, though you may well wish to read it all at once. Secondly, babies develop at very different rates. Some will be crawling at eight months and others not until twelve months or later; some babies will be sitting up at five months and others not until nine months. Some babies are physically very active and mobile, others concentrate more on how to use their hands or on learning to speak early. So don't be worried if your baby isn't doing what it says on that particular week; it doesn't mean he or she is in any way abnormal!

Cross-references are included wherever necessary, and at the back of the book is a full index, to help you look up information on a particular topic if you do not find it in the week that seems appropriate to your baby.

At regular intervals in the book you will find information on how and what to feed your baby. This follows the recommendations now made by pediatricians on what is best for a growing baby. Of course, you can vary this if you have good cause – always discuss your reasons for weaning or any change in diet with your doctor or health provider.

You can use the space on the left-hand pages to write down appointments and reminders of things you have to do, as well as to keep a note of your feelings. You can also use it to keep a record of your baby's progress, recording the day he first smiles or learns to crawl or when he takes his first dramatic steps. The book is also meant to give you tips and information which will help remind you when your baby needs his first vaccinations, for example, or when you should let your employer know whether you intend to return to work or not.

First Year, Week by Week is aimed not only at mothers but at both the baby's parents. Modern fathers have a wonderful opportunity to learn to share in the joys and the hard work of parenthood. If you are a working mother, it is even more important that your partner shares in household tasks and helps care for the baby as well as providing another source of security and fun.

Above all, we believe that looking after your baby should be fun as well as, inevitably, being hard work and a great responsibility. So we have included ideas for games and activities which you can enjoy with the baby at various different stages in his or her development.

The baby is referred to as 'he' or 'she' in alternate chapters throughout the book to reflect the fact that the text applies equally to male and female children. The term 'partner' has been chosen to cover the baby's father, no matter what his status.

There is a list of useful addresses at the end of the book. Refer to the groups or associations if you would like more information about a particular aspect whose detailed coverage is beyond the scope of this book.

A note about the author
Maggie Jones's second child had just celebrated his first birthday when she started to write this book, so all the problems and rewards of a baby's first precious year were fresh in her mind as she wrote. Like many babies, hers did not behave as most of the baby books assume they should, and she frequently found herself wondering what on earth to try next!

She intends in this book to share some of the tips and solutions to their problems that she and other mothers found, as well as providing practical information. She hopes also to convey some of the pleasures, as well as the hard work, of bringing up a baby.

Maggie Jones is, sadly, now 39. She has three children.

week 1

month _____ *date* _____

MON

_____

TUES

_____

WED

_____

THURS

_____

FRI

_____

SAT

_____

SUN

_____

When you pick your new baby up, always take care to support his head. Babies like to be held closely and handled confidently – this makes them feel secure. Hold your baby against your shoulder, supporting his head, or cradled in your arm so that he can look up at your face.

Most new mothers and fathers are afraid of dropping their babies or of harming them by mistake, and may also be nervous about changing and bathing them. Remember that a baby will sense your nervousness and that it is therefore important to handle him firmly but gently; talk to your baby to reassure him too.

When you pick your baby up, slip your hand under his head to prevent it from flopping backwards, and use the other hand to support his body.

Many babies like to be carried with their head resting on your shoulder. Use one hand to support his bottom and the other to prevent his head from flopping back.

*n*OTES

Don't forget You should schedule your baby's first checkup with the pediatrician or family doctor. Keep important phone numbers posted by your telephone, for safety and convenience.

*f*EEDING YOUR BABY

*t*he main concern of every new mother is how to feed her baby. Most mothers will know that breast-feeding is best for their babies. Not only is a mother's milk perfectly adapted for the baby's needs, it also contains antibodies to infections which will protect him in the early weeks.

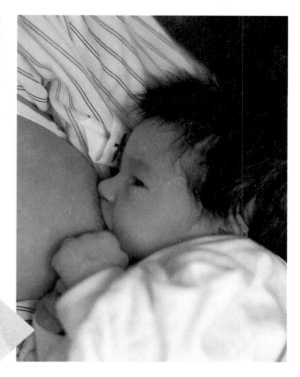

If you touch your baby's cheek with your breast he will automatically turn his head towards the breast and open his mouth, ready to feed.

FACTS ABOUT FEEDING

If you want to breast-feed, it is important that the baby is put to the breast as soon as possible after delivery. For the first few days the breasts produce a yellowish substance called colostrum, which is rich in protein and antibodies. The mature milk generally comes in on the third or fourth day after the birth, and usually looks rather watery.

Some mothers find that their nipples get sore to begin with and their breasts may be painful when the milk first comes in. Some babies are slow to get the idea of breast-feeding and may take some time to get 'latched on' properly. Unless he is correctly latched on, your nipples will get

sore and the baby will not get enough milk. Remember to start each feeding on a different breast.

Your doctor or midwife will be helpful in sorting out any initial problems, either at the hospital or once you get home. The La Leche League also has breast-feeding counselors who will help (see Week 7).

Some women experience more difficulties than others in breast-feeding and some just do not enjoy it. Don't feel guilty if you decide to bottle-feed: most babies will thrive on formula milk. What your baby needs most is love and attention, so make sure he is getting plenty of both.

It is very important that all equipment used for bottle-feeding (whether you are giving formula or expressed milk or cooled, boiled water) is thoroughly washed and sterilized.

Breast-fed babies may feed very often, sometimes as much as every two hours and some need ten to twelve feedings in 24 hours. Many mothers worry that their breast-milk is inadequate and consider whether they should supplement with formula. The truth is that the more frequently the baby nurses, the more milk the breasts will produce. As the baby gets bigger he will take more milk at each feeding and need to feed less often.

week 2

month   date

MON

TUES

WED

THURS

FRI

SAT

SUN

THE BABY'S APPEARANCE

The newborn baby may appear less attractive than your imaginings in the days after the birth. Her head may look swollen or lumpy in places after the delivery. Some babies' skin peels a lot or may still have some of the protective substance called vernix on it; other babies have skin rashes or may be born with hair on parts of their bodies.

The umbilical cord area should merely be kept clean and dry, so it doesn't become infected. The baby's breasts or genitals may seem swollen after the birth due to the mother's hormones getting into her bloodstream during birth. This will soon clear up.

The umbilical cord is cut quite short and securely clamped. It soon begins to dry and shrivel.

It usually drops off within ten days or so, but it may go black and bleed a little.

nOTES

Don't forget Ask your doctor whether you need to make an appointment for your baby's first Hepatitus B shot.

*f*or many mothers the idea of coping with the baby on their own can seem quite frightening. Also, most babies sleep a lot during the 48 hours after the birth, and going home from the hospital may coincide with her having wakeful periods or crying a lot. This can make the new mother feel she is doing something wrong.

Remember that your pediatrician or family practitioner is there to help you if you have any questions about your baby's health or general care. If you are calling because you believe your baby may be ill, make a list of significant points before you call: Does your baby have a temperature? Has there been a change in the amount she has eaten recently? Is she irritable or lethargic? Is she pale or flushed? How frequent or infrequent have her bowel movements been?

Most newborn babies will have fretful periods in the day or evening; if you are breast-feeding, do not automatically assume that she is crying because she is still hungry. A newborn baby will root around for the breast even when not hungry because the breast is her main source of comfort. If your baby is crying for no apparent reason, and has been fed recently, try walking around with her in a carrier or sling or held close to the body, or swaddle her and rock her in a carriage or cradle. A lullaby tape or a music box may have a soothing effect. Some small babies are unusually wakeful and may just like to be walked around rather than left in their cradle.

In the first few days, try to get friends, relatives or your partner to cope with all the necessary chores in the house while you concentrate on yourself and the baby, and on getting the rest you need.

'POSTNATAL BLUES'

Many mothers feel weepy and emotional in the first days or weeks after the birth. Some women find they have a weepy period around the third or fourth day, which is when the milk comes in; this can be partly explained by the changing hormone levels in your body.

You may find getting back to your normal routines at home stressful in itself, especially if the house is untidy or disorganized and there is work to do. Visitors can also prove too much at times, especially if you were wanting some time to yourself. Don't be afraid of saying 'I must rest now' when the baby has gone to sleep. At least make a rule that visitors make the coffee and clean up afterwards.

Occasionally a mother continues to feel depressed or weepy after the birth of a baby, and may need to talk this over with a doctor or counselor.

week 3

MON

TUES

WED

THURS

April 20th
FRI
1st smile

SAT

SUN

*n*OTES

DRESSING BABY

All-in-one stretch suits with snaps at the front and crotch are the easiest for changing a baby. Many parents prefer these to nightgowns which tend to ride up and leave the baby exposed, although some gowns tie or have snaps at the bottom.

With all clothes, make sure sleeves are not too tight, that there is plenty of room for him to kick, and that there is nothing itchy next to his skin.

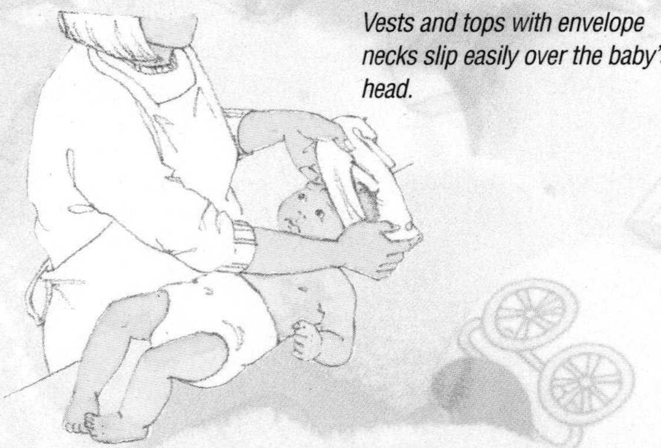

Vests and tops with envelope necks slip easily over the baby's head.

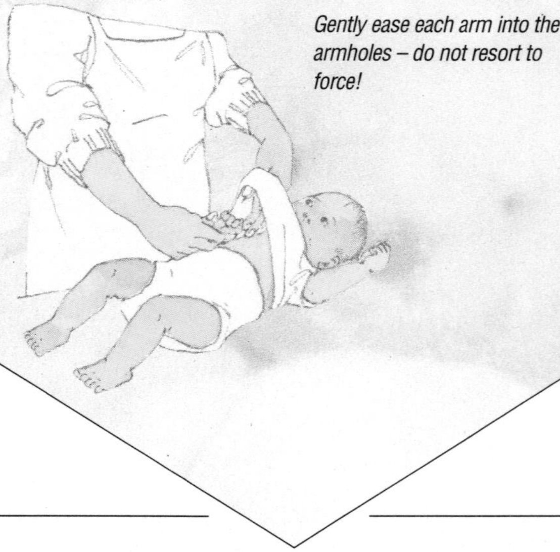

Gently ease each arm into the armholes – do not resort to force!

Don't forget Mothers, Fathers, and Child-Care Providers need to be up-to-date with their immunizations. All adults should have a DPT booster every ten years. Women of childbearing age need to have a blood test to check their immunity to rubella.

*C*LOTHES AND EQUIPMENT

t here is such a bewildering array of goods on sale that it's hard to make the right choice. Friends and relatives will give you clothes for the baby, so just buy the essential garments to begin with and wait to see what else you need.

You will need several changes of clothes for your baby because diapers often leak and some dribbling and regurgitating of milk is inevitable. Clothes made from natural fibers are best for young babies. Don't buy too many small sizes as these will quickly be outgrown. A good basic wardrobe includes four undershirts, four to six stretch suits or nightgowns, one or two blanket-sleepers, one or two sweaters, snowsuit, mittens and hat for a winter baby, cotton hat and booties for summer.

The basic immediate requirements for equipment are somewhere for the baby to sleep and some form of transportation. To prevent serious injury, infants should be in a safety seat when riding in a car. When acquiring a safety seat, be certain it has a label indicating that it meets or exceeds Federal Motor Vehicle Safety Standard (FMVSS) 213.

There is no immediate need for a full-size crib. The stroller or bassinet or a Moses basket will do for the first six weeks. If you inherit or buy equipment secondhand, always check they are safe. You can always call the U.S. Consumer Product Safety Commission Hotline (1-800-638-2772) to check on which models of furniture or equipment have been recalled.

See Week 4 for Diapers

See Week 5 for Bathing Baby

See Week 11 for Choosing a Crib

TRANSPORTATION

The choice of equipment for transporting your baby includes an all-in-one system incorporating a portable bassinet on a carriage frame, a bassinet or traveller body on a foldaway transporter chassis, a pushchair and a sling or baby carrier.

SLEEPING

A Moses basket is useful, as you can carry it around the house, but it cannot be safely secured in a car. Infants who weigh up to 20 pounds (about one year old) should use an infant-only or other safety seat in the rear-facing position.

11

week 4

month   *date*

MON

_____

TUES

_____

WED

_____

THURS

_____

FRI

_____

SAT

_____

SUN

_____

*n*OTES

SLEEPING SAFELY

Most babies will adopt a favorite position to sleep in, but, until they are old enough to roll over, they will depend on you to put them down so that they are comfortable. The safest position for a young baby to sleep in, is on his back or side, not his tummy.

The latest guidelines on crib death stress the importance of sleeping position in reducing the risk of a crib death. The risk can be reduced if babies are not placed on their tummies when they are going to sleep.

Keep the temperature in your baby's room so that you feel comfortable in it (65°F). Babies should not be allowed to get too warm or too cold.

Babies should always lie on firm, flat surfaces, not on pillows or soft, fluffy comforters or sheepskin rugs. Use lightweight blankets which you can add or take away according to the room temperature.

Put the baby down on her side, with the lower arm forward to prevent her rolling over.

Babies can be laid down to sleep on their backs.

Don't forget Your baby should be in a smoke-free environment. Keep smokers away!

*n*ew mothers are often uncertain whether to opt for disposable diapers or cloth ones. Choosing cloth diapers seems a big initial outlay; as well as the diapers you also need a bucket for soaking, the sterilizing solution, diaper liners, plastic pants and diaper pins. However, cloth diapers do work out cheaper in the long run, and many mothers find them more efficient at keeping a young baby dry.

The decision will depend largely on your circumstances. If you have a washer and dryer or easy access to them, then cloth diapers may well be best. Some mothers find that cloth diapers are more absorbent, especially for a small breast-fed baby, and that they therefore have fewer baby clothes to wash. Cloth diapers may seem difficult to put on at first, but it doesn't take long once you're used to it – even in the dark in the middle of the night.

If you don't have much space and washing is a problem, disposable diapers are the more practical solution. Try out several different kinds and make sure they don't irritate your baby's bottom. Elasticated legs are a good idea for small babies. Modern disposables are convenient, very absorbent and are less bulky than cloth diapers. There are also special designs produced for girls and boys.

Changing diapers can be done quickly if you can have everything in one place near to the changing mat or table. Make sure that cleaning materials, cream and fresh diapers and liners are to hand. If you are using cloth diapers, keep the diaper bucket nearby.

1 Wipe the baby's bottom and then use absorbent cotton and warm water or a baby wipe to cleanse her skin. Clean and dry thoroughly in the folds or the skin may get sore.

2 Use zinc and castor oil cream or another preparation to protect the skin. If a rash develops, ask your doctor for advice.

3 Put on a clean diaper, fastening the sticky tape of a disposable diaper at the front. (Remember to wipe a girl from front to back to prevent bacteria spreading from the anus, infecting the vagina.)

NIGHT CHANGING

Many babies soil their diapers after a feeding. If you change the diaper first, the baby may go back to sleep after her feeding but with a dirty diaper; if you change it after the feeding, you may wake her up. Most babies settle into a pattern quite quickly. You can get special thick cloth diapers or disposables, and one-way diaper liners, for nighttime use.

If you change a diaper quickly and keep the room dark, you won't disturb her very much and this may prevent her getting sore. Breast-fed babies are much less prone to diaper rash.

week 5

month _____ date _____

MON _____

TUES _____

WED _____

THURS _____

FRI _____

SAT _____

SUN

May 6th
1st airplane ride
to N.Y.

𝑛OTES

By five or six weeks your new baby should be rewarding you with his first smile. He will look at you and study your face first, before breaking into a smile; you need to talk to him and give him a chance to respond.

A small baby at this stage will also 'fix' his gaze on an object and follow it if it moves. The human face is what he most enjoys looking at and he will 'fix' on your face for quite long periods.

When your newborn baby hears your voice he may turn his eyes towards the sound and will follow your face if you hold it close to his.

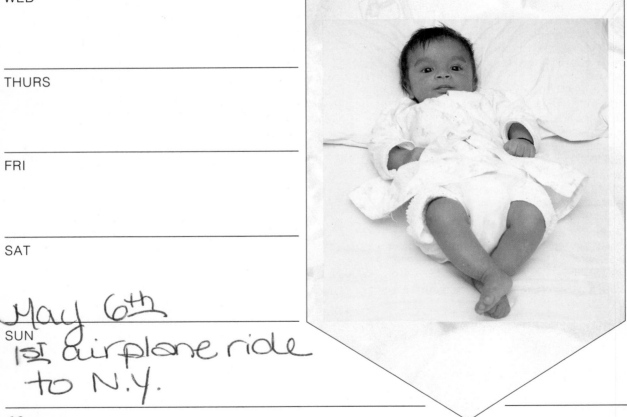

Don't forget Note the date of your baby's first smile. Make an appointment for your postpartum checkup if you haven't already done so.

ᑲATHING BABY

ᑲathing the baby can initially be a traumatic time for some new parents, especially if he screams, writhes and thrashes. Once he enjoys his bath, however, it is a delightful form of exercise for him.

New babies do not need bathing every day, especially if they hate it. 'Sponge bathing' will keep a baby clean in the early weeks if you can't give a bath. But try to bath him every few days to give him a chance to get used to it.

It helps to get everything ready first and to bath the baby somewhere where you will be warm and comfortable. A baby bath with stand brings the baby to the right height, but you could bath him on a firm table or other surface provided you do not turn your back for a moment.

Make sure the water is about body temperature (it shouldn't feel hot or cold if you dip your elbow in) and hold the baby firmly, talking to him all the time. Many babies dislike getting undressed but are quiet in the water.

If your baby really does hate the bath, you can try having him in the bath with you provided there's someone else around to help pass the baby in and out. Let your bath water cool right down. Most babies will find the skin-to-skin contact reassuring and this may help them get over their fear of the water.

Many parents find that a bath makes a pleasant end to the day, and also tires the baby out. However, if you have older children, the morning may be a better time for bathing him; he will probably then settle down for a long morning sleep. Evening bathtime also enables fathers to be involved with the baby.

1 With your baby wrapped in a towel, hold his head over the bath and wash his scalp gently with your free hand. Pat it dry.

2 Support his head with your forearm and let him splash for a few minutes, rather than soaping him right away.

3 Have a warm towel ready to wrap the baby in when he comes out, as small babies get cold very quickly.

A SPONGE BATH

Hold the baby safely and gently clean his face with absorbent cotton and warm water. Wipe his eyes first, from the bridge of the nose outwards, using a different piece for each eye so as not to spread any infection. Wipe around the ears with absorbent cotton. Then clean up the rest of his face to remove traces of milk or saliva which may irritate his skin. Pat dry with a soft towel. Wash his hands and clean his bottom. Dry well and put on a fresh diaper.

See Week 4 for Diapers

week 6

month May 14th _date_

MON
1ST day of daycare

TUES

WED

THURS

FRI

SAT

SUN

_n_OTES

ROUTINE LABORATORY TESTS

In the normal process of growing up, your child will probably need various kinds of medical services, ranging from routine physical examinations (see 'Well-baby examinations,' p. 19) to laboratory tests to surgery. Some of the laboratory tests commonly performed:

Lead screening Some pediatricians recommend this blood test be done between nine months and one-year of age.

CBC (Complete blood count) Some pediatricians recommend that this test be done between nine months and one-year of age to establish a baseline.

Tuberculosis screening (the Tine test) Many pediatricians recommend that it be done at one-year of age and then at every routine physical examination.

Cholesterol screening A blood test performed after age five.

Urine screening Usually starts at age two.

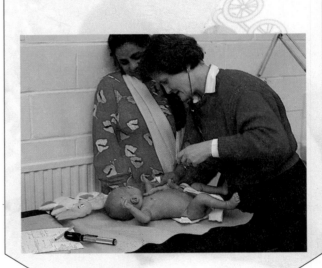

Don't forget Your health is vital to the well-being of your baby. If you have problems or worries, don't be afraid to talk about them.

*t*HE POSTNATAL CHECKUP

*Y*ou will need to have a postnatal checkup about six weeks after the birth. The doctor will feel your abdomen to check that the womb has returned to its normal size and may check your weight, urine and blood pressure. You will be asked if you have had any unusual pain, bleeding or discharge; it is quite normal for the lochia, the usual discharge after the baby's birth, to still be present. Your doctor will probably do a Pap smear test.

If you still have pain in the site of your episiotomy, make sure the doctor checks to ensure that it is not infected. The doctor may also look at your breasts and nipples if you are having problems with breast-feeding. The doctor will usually discuss contraception with you at this visit.

The postnatal checkup gives you the opportunity to discuss any worries you might have. You may be anxious about sex if you have either tried intercourse and found it painful or have not yet attempted it, which is very common.

THE BIRTH CERTIFICATE

There will be many occasions in the coming years when you will need a certified birth certificate for your child; for example, when you register your child for school. In order to obtain a certified birth certificate with an official raised seal, you must write either to your state Bureau of Vital Statistics (usually located in the state capital) or to the registry office in the town or borough where your child was born. In your letter, supply the child's name, date and place of birth, father's name, mother's maiden name, and your current address.

POSTNATAL EXERCISES

Many mothers find they are so busy after the birth that they are tempted to give up doing postnatal exercises after a week or two. It is important that you carry on with these exercises as they will help you keep fit and make you better able to enjoy your baby. Below is a reminder of some of the basic exercises which you should do several times a day.

See Week 7 for Well-baby examinations

STOMACH MUSCLES
Lie on your back on the floor, knees bent and hands on upper chest. Lift your head and shoulders off the floor, keeping your waist and back on the floor: look at your knees. Then relax.

BACK STRENGTHENING
Lie face downwards on the floor, arms behind your back, clasping hands loosely. Lift your head and shoulders off the floor. Then relax.

PELVIC FLOOR MUSCLES
Tighten the muscles to pull up your vagina and anus towards your body. Hold for five seconds and then relax. If you are not sure that you are tightening the right muscles, try interrupting the flow of urine the next time you pee.

Do this exercise regularly; it is very important as it will help you avoid problems such as prolapse of the uterus, or incontinence.

See Week 23 for Keeping Fit

week 7

month   date

MON

TUES

WED

THURS

FRI

SAT

SUN

NOTES

WHAT BABY CAN SEE

Babies can see immediately after birth, although they initially only focus within a very narrow range. A baby can focus on objects held within 10in (25cm) of his face. Despite his limited focusing, a baby will flinch or try to protect himself if you move something rapidly towards him.

Your baby cannot see colors at all to begin with. As the first colors he will respond to will be bright ones, give him brightly colored objects to look at.

WELL-BABY EXAMINATIONS

*W*ell-baby visits to the doctor during the first-year are extremely important. At these visits, your baby is given careful physical examinations, routine tests, and those necessary immunizations (see 'First Immunizations', p. 21). These visits also provide an excellent opportunity for you to air your concerns. The first visit is usually scheduled the first two weeks after birth. Some doctors require at least three more visits in the first year and two in the second; others like to see infants on a monthly basis for the first six months. Of course, you should not hesitate to phone your doctor between visits if your baby becomes ill or you have additional concerns.

See Week 1 for Feeding Your Baby

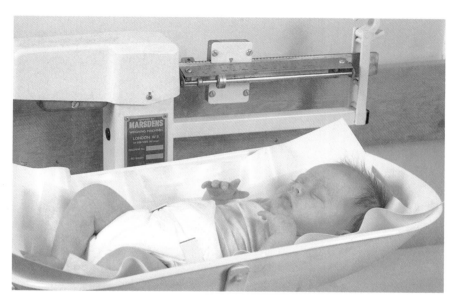

HELP AND ADVICE

You usually have to undress the baby to be weighed, so it is important to put him in clothes that will come off easily; also take a spare diaper in case you need to change him. The nurse will enter the baby's weight both in their records and in a book which you keep with you. A baby's weight may vary according to whether he has just had a bowel movement or not, so don't take each week's gain too seriously if the trend is good.

Most doctors are very supportive of breast-feeding and will give you advice if your breast-fed baby is not gaining weight satisfactorily or if you have other problems. However, you may feel you need extra help or advice with breast-feeding, in which case ask for the name of the local La Leche League breast-feeding counselor. These counselors are trained mothers who have breast-fed their own babies and will be dedicated to helping you to breast-feed if this is what you want.

Your doctor will advise you about giving vitamin supplements (usually not until six months) or fluoride drops to help create strong, healthy teeth. They will also help with other problems such as colic or lack of sleep and first illnesses such as colds.

The doctor's office can also be a good place to chat to other mothers and make new friends. Some doctors' offices display information about local mother and baby groups and other activities for mothers and their young children. Some also have a bulletinboard where secondhand baby clothes and equipment are advertised or where you can advertise for babysitters when you go back to work.

week 8

month   date

MON

TUES

WED

THURS

FRI

SAT

SUN

notes

Your baby will now be spending more time awake during the daytime and you will be wondering how to divert her. From six weeks on you can sit her in a bouncing cradle and move her from room to room with you so she can watch you as you work. Never put the cradle on a high surface as the baby's movements could easily shift it.

With the baby in a carrier or sling, you can keep her close to you while you do tasks around the house. Many parents find a sling particularly valuable for carrying a crying baby around, leaving both arms free while at the same time giving the baby comfort and security.

You can also take your baby round the house in her infant seat so that you can talk to her while you work.

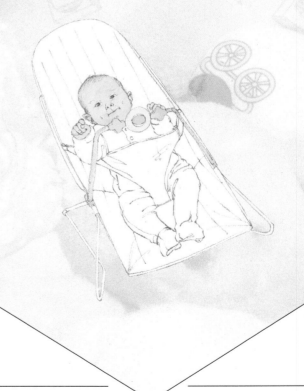

ƒIRST IMMUNIZATIONS

by immunizing your child, you are not only protecting her but, by reducing the number of people who catch such diseases, you are also protecting your next baby and other people's children who have not been immunized. Because diseases like polio and diphtheria have become so rare, some people have become careless about having their children immunized. If fewer people have their children immunized, it becomes more likely that these diseases will reappear.

Now at birth, or shortly thereafter, the American Academy of Pediatrics recommends that children begin a series of three innoculations against the Hepatitus B virus, which is highly contagious and can cause serious liver damage. Starting at two months of age, the other usual series of vaccinations begin – the polio vaccine (given by mouth) and the 'triple vaccine' for diptheria, tetanus, and whooping cough (pertussis). These are repeated at four months and then again at six months (DTP and HIB only).

The vaccines should not cause any side-effects, except perhaps for a reddish patch at the site of the injection and occasionally a temperature. The whooping cough vaccine can very rarely cause serious side-effects, such as a fit or convulsion leading to brain damage. It is important though to remember that whooping cough is a serious disease which itself can lead to brain damage or even death. You will be advised not to have the whooping cough vaccine if there is a history of epilepsy or convulsions in the baby's immediate family or if she has already suffered a fit herself.

At the same time, your baby will be given the Hib injection. (Hib is short for Haemophilus influenzae type b, a bacteria which causes a range of illnesses.) The injection immunizes against, among other things, croup and some forms of meningitis and pneumonia.

Tuberculosis is still common in some parts of the country, and children are highly susceptible to this contagious disease. It is recommended that children be tested for tuberculosis (the Tine test) at one-year of age and then at routine physicals. All adult family members of children with positive TB tests should also be tested.

Some time after your baby's first birthday you will be advised that she should have the combined measles, mumps and rubella vaccine (MMR). Measles, for example, can be a very unpleasant illness and sometimes has serious consequences, such as ear infections and pneumonia. When your baby is immunized you can discuss the MMR vaccine too.

If you have any worries about your baby's immunizations do discuss these with the doctor. It's wise to keep a record (signed by your doctor) of all your child's immunizations.

IMMUNIZATION TIMETABLE

Birth	●	1st Hepatitus B
1 month	●	2nd Hepatitus B
2 months	●	1st DTP; 1st OPV (oral polio vaccine); 1st HIB
4 months	●	2nd DTP, OPV, and HIB
6 months	●	3rd DTP and HIB; 3rd Hepatitus B
15 months	●	MMR; booster HIB

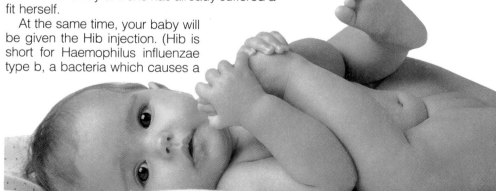

week 9

month   *date*

MON

June 5th

TUES

rolled over
front to back

WED

June   7th

THURS

2 month old shots
done

FRI

SAT

SUN

HEAD CONTROL

Your baby will gradually learn to control his head and be able to lift it for longer periods. You may find that he bumps his head against your shoulder while you are carrying him as he practices his head control.

When lying on his tummy he will start to lift his head up at a 45-degree angle and look straight ahead for a few minutes at a time. Until your baby has gained full head control, continue to support his head.

By two months your baby will probably be able to lift his head up for several minutes, using his forearms as support.

By three or four months he will be able to do 'push-ups' and may also make crawling movements with his arms and legs.

Don't forget Check that you have made an appointment for your baby's next 'well-baby' visit.

*n*OTES

OUT AND ABOUT

$g$etting out of the house may seem a major undertaking at first. A short trip to the store is not too much of a problem but if you are going further afield you may wonder if it is worth the effort. The baby needs to be fed and changed; then a change of clothes, spare diapers and bottles if you are bottle-feeding need to be packed.

It helps if you keep a bag ready containing everything you need, so that you can just pick it up as you leave the house. If you are traveling by car, always keep a spare change in the car so that you won't be caught without diapers or clothes. Even if you usually use cloth diapers, disposables are handy for going out so that you don't have to carry a bag of dirty, perhaps smelly, diapers around with you.

Breast-feeding mothers have an advantage over bottle-feeding mothers because they don't need to take feeding equipment with them, but some women are anxious about having to breast-feed their baby in public. There are far too few public places in which to feed babies comfortably and privately. However, it is possible to breast-feed discreetly if you wear suitable clothing, including a large scarf perhaps.

If you take your baby out by car, you are required by law to use a child safety seat. Make sure you read the instructions that come with the safety seat as well as your vehicle's owner's manual on proper safety seat installation. Infants placed in improperly installed safety seats have been known to die in crashes. Infant safety seats must be used in a rear-facing position. However, infant seats should not be placed on the front passenger side in air-bag equipped cars; they should be placed in a rear-facing position in the back of the vehicle. Make sure the safety seat's strap is snug.

> If you use public transportation, it is easiest if you take a stroller which folds up or else carry the baby in a sling or carrier.

YOUR CLOTHES

As a new mother you will find it hard to look good and feel comfortable at the same time. Buy a few well-chosen clothes if you are still too big to get back into pre-pregnancy clothes and are tired of maternity clothes.

Clothes that are practical and comfortable do not have to be dowdy – looking good will help you to feel that you are coping as well as making you feel attractive. Buy clothes that wash and iron easily.

Breast-feeding mothers will want either front-opening clothes or loose tops which they can pull up to feed the baby more discreetly – and comfortable skirts or trousers. In winter, a wrap will keep you both warm.

week 10

month   **date**

MON

TUES

WED

THURS

FRI

SAT

SUN

Crying is the only way a small baby can communicate her feelings. A baby usually has a reason for crying and, although at first it is difficult to distinguish between different cries, you will soon begin to recognize variations and to guess her needs more accurately (see Week 19). However, some young babies do cry more than others, seemingly for comfort or distraction.

If your baby cries a lot, she will need to be soothed. Try putting her in a sling and carrying her round with you: you can make a sling out of a large shawl if necessary. Holding her firmly against your shoulder and rocking her or walking up and down are good ways of soothing a crying baby, especially if she tends to thrash around. Motion is soothing. You can use a rocking cradle or rock the pram.

Take solace, if you can, in the fact that by the time most babies are three-months old those periods of irritable crying have stopped. In the meantime, take care of yourself. Hire a sitter or ask a friend or neighbor to come in and relieve you so you can get out.

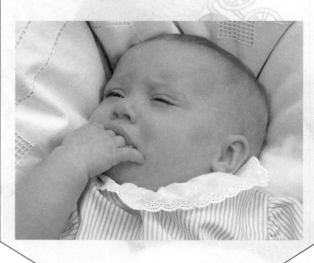

*n*OTES

BABY'S FIRST ILLNESS

*Y*ou will be very lucky if you get through the baby's first few months without a minor illness – even though a breast-fed baby is protected by your antibodies to illnesses which you have had. New parents worry about their baby and the fear that they might appear to be over-anxious can deter them from taking the baby to the doctor. However, no doctor will mind seeing a small baby, even if it turns out not to be serious. Your need for reassurance is a very natural response.

- Almost all babies will pick up a cold in the early months of their life, and occasionally something more serious. A cold can cause problems in feeding if her nose is very blocked and she cannot suck well. If this happens, the doctor or nurse may recommend a decongestant to enable her to breathe more easily. At night, try propping up the head of the crib or use a cool-mist humidifier to relieve some of her congestion.
- Many babies have a slight rash called a milk rash which does no harm at all, and looks like tiny pimples on the skin. A red, scaly rash, which may weep and irritate, is more likely to be eczema, which can be caused or exacerbated by an allergy.
- Diaper rash is caused by bacteria in the baby's stools breaking down the urine into ammonia, which damages the skin. A very red blotchy rash in the diaper area may be caused by thrush; this can only be cured by an antifungal medicine which your doctor can prescribe.
- Many babies cry a great deal in the early weeks. Some have a pattern of 'evening crying', others may have crying spells at other times of the day or even all day long. Many such babies are said to suffer from colic, although nobody really knows what colic is. Some attribute it to the baby's immature nervous system. Others assume that it is caused by indigestion-type pains in the intestine. However, many colicky babies appear to need very little sleep and their crying seems to be related more to lack of sleep than feeding. Colicky babies usually gain weight well, are healthy and grow out of their colicky spells by three to six months. The parents of colicky babies are often more in need of help, as this can be a stressful time.
- A baby who is really ill, surprisingly, cries little but seems listless, has little appetite, may not gain weight well and/or may have vomiting and diarrhea; she will not be interested in what is going on around her.
- Take your baby to the doctor if she runs a high temperature, is breathing rapidly, vomits large amounts of milk, has watery diarrhea, has a bad cough or appears in pain.

TAKING TEMPERATURE AND GIVING MEDICINE

You can take the baby's temperature with a thermometer held under the armpit. Put the bulb of the thermometer in her armpit and hold her arm against her side for two minutes. You can do this while feeding to distract her if she struggles.

You can alternatively use a fever strip, which changes color depending on the baby's temperature, though this gives a less accurate reading.

Giving medicine by spoon can be tricky, both with a small baby who is not used to spoons, and with a larger one who dislikes the taste. If you cannot get the baby to take medicine off an ordinary spoon, try giving it in a special tube-shaped, non-spill medicine 'spoon' or a dropper which is sterilized.

week 11

month   date

MON

TUES

WED

THURS

FRI

SAT

SUN

COMFORT OBJECTS

Your baby may become very attached to a 'comforter' such as a special soft toy or a blanket. As long as he uses these only when needed and does not withdraw from other activities, they will do no harm and may be a bonus in helping him to go to sleep without tears.

If you have used a pacifier, your baby may rely on one to get him to sleep. This won't do him any harm either, but if you want to break the habit, it might be easier to provide another security object now rather than later. Some babies wake frequently in the night because the pacifier drops out and they need you to come and pop it back in!

Some babies suck their thumbs or fingers for comfort and this habit is almost impossible to stop. Many parents welcome this habit as it usually means peaceful bedtimes, and there is no need to discourage it, provided he sucks his thumb to get to sleep, and not too much in the day.

nOTES

Don't forget A pacifier needs to be sterilized too.

SLEEP PATTERNS

*M*ost parents hope that by about three or four months their baby will be sleeping through the night, but many are not. Some babies, perhaps because of teething problems or a cold, or because they need comfort, develop a habit of waking regularly again in the night.

WAYS TO DEVELOP SLEEP PATTERNS

It may help to make a clear division between night and day. During the day naps may be taken in a carriage or portable crib downstairs, but at night he sleeps in his crib in a darkened room. In the daytime you might go immediately to your baby when he wakes and cries, but at night give him a few minutes to settle down first. If your baby is a light sleeper, make sure he is not disturbed by the family going to bed. Light sleepers do better in their own room.

Every child – and adult too – wakes briefly at regular intervals during the night. Many babies wake briefly and, finding themselves alone, immediately cry. If they have gone to sleep sucking at the breast or bottle they may cry for its return. Such babies may go on demanding nighttime feedings long after they have ceased to be necessary.

Encourage your baby to learn to fall asleep on his own in his crib. If he cries, go back in after a few minutes, resettle him, and leave him to fall asleep.

Some parents find it easier to settle the baby if they take him straight into their bed. Provided they know this habit may be hard to break, and do not resent sharing a bed, this can be the answer till the baby is old enough to sleep alone.

Some babies wake very early in the morning. Check that the room is warm enough and that curtains exclude light effectively. If you cannot juggle his bedtime so that he sleeps later in the morning, at least put interesting things in the crib for him to look at such as an 'activity center'.

See Week 40 for Sleep Problems

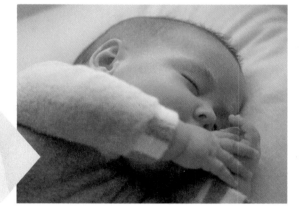

Babies vary a lot in their need for sleep and some are lighter sleepers than others. It does no harm to the baby if he wakes several times a night but, if you are exhausted, you may feel that you are not enjoying your baby as you should.

CHOOSING A CRIB

You can buy a crib that converts to a junior bed; these are less expensive than a regular crib and may be used up to age five. A standard crib can be used from birth up to about two-and-a-half years, or whenever the baby learns to climb out of it. All cribs must have slats no further apart than $2\frac{3}{8}$ inches, tight-fitting mattresses, corner posts less than $\frac{5}{8}$ inches tall, at least 26 inches from the top of the rail to the mattress set at its lowest level, childproof side locking mechanisms, and be painted only with lead-free paint.

If you inherit a crib from family or friends or acquire one at a garage sale or secondhand shop, check with the U.S. Consumer Product Safety Commission Hotline (1-800-638-2772) to make sure it hasn't been recalled.

week 12

month   *date*

MON

TUES

WED

THURS

FRI

SAT

SUN

𝑛OTES

SOCIAL DEVELOPMENT

By three months your baby will already be a social person, taking her greatest pleasure out of her relationship with you. She will laugh when you tickle or talk to her and will love being tickled when you change her diaper.

At this age your baby is likely to stop crying when she hears your voice or when you pick her up. She also responds to other people who pay her attention with smiles and by kicking and waving her arms, although her greatest enthusiasm is likely to be reserved for her mother.

Don't forget It is important to continue with your pelvic floor exercises.

yOU AND YOUR PARTNER

*i*f you have both been going out to work and shared equally in household tasks, you may find that things are different now that you are at home with your baby. Your partner may assume that, because you are at home, responsibility for household tasks falls more on your shoulders now and he can relax. If you have always played a domestic role, you may feel that it is all too much to cope with at once.

In the early weeks you may be totally pre-occupied with the baby, and your partner may not understand why you have so little time to talk to him or be with him. Even though he realizes that the baby's demands must come first, he may start to feel left out or be worried that things will never be the same between you.

A partner really has two choices when he has a new baby. He can either involve himself with the baby, take over some of the tasks, like changing diapers, bathing, feeding a bottle-fed baby and comforting her when she cries – or he can sit back and let the mother do the major part. If he

involves himself with the baby, he will realize how demanding a baby is and will better understand why his partner is so tired. If, however, he does not involve himself with the baby, he may feel left out and might become resentful of his partner's tiredness and seeming lack of interest in him – and wish that things could get 'back to normal' as soon as possible.

See Week 14
for Leaving
Baby at Home

See Week 21
for Fathers

It is important that you and your partner try to create some time for each other and that you do talk things over. Once the baby is old enough to be left with a trusted baby-sitter you can go out by yourselves, or you may be able to find time to be together when the baby is asleep, postponing chores until later.

RESUMING SEX

Sex is often a problem at this time. After the discomforts of pregnancy and the birth, many women are anxious that they may not feel comfortable or they may want affection and cuddles rather than passion. Many men see no reason why making love

should be postponed any longer.

Unless a couple can talk openly about their feelings, resentment can build up. It can help to talk about it to your doctor or a counselor. A permanent loss of interest in sex

can be a symptom of depression but is perfectly understandable so soon after giving birth. Some mothers are simply afraid of how sex after childbirth will feel, or they fear that their partners will no longer find them attractive.

week 13

month	date

MON

TUES

WED

THURS

FRI

SAT

SUN

*n*OTES

By two to two-and-a-half months, your baby will become fascinated watching his hands moving and will move them in front of his face. By three months he will be very interested in 'measuring' the distance between objects and himself, which is when he begins reaching out and swiping at those within his reach.

By three to four months you will need to be on your guard because your baby will start to grab at everything within reach, and will have a preference for things that move and make a noise.

Many two-month-old babies will lie for long periods watching their hands move. They will also be fascinated by mobiles wafting in the air.

By three months your baby will take great pleasure in swiping with his fists at anything within reach.

CLOTHING AND TOYS

s your baby grows and you go out more together he will probably need more clothes. He may require warmer, thicker stretch suits or jogging suits for daytime wear in the winter, or larger woollen jackets and sweaters. If it is cold, a snowsuit will keep the baby warm and dry outdoors, without wrapping him under layers of blankets in a carriage.

Don't make the mistake of overdressing your baby, especially when he is in a warm house. As babies get bigger they do learn to adjust to warm or cold conditions. Always wrap him up warmly when going out in the cold, however; hats are very important as most of a baby's heat loss is through his head. When you come into a warm house or a heated public place, always unwrap your baby, even if he is fast asleep. Blankets wrapped around him will be less disturbing. When you come in out of the rain, pull back any plastic covers so he is comfortable.

Many babies overheat easily and can readily develop a heat rash, so be sure not to put too many clothes on a summer baby if the weather is hot. Babies have cold hands and feet most of the time, so feel the back of his neck if you want to check how warm he is.

FIRST TOYS

Your baby will be starting to take more interest in the objects around him. He will love to watch brightly colored mobiles. He will reach out for things he can see and will enjoy swiping at them.

It will be another few weeks before your baby can actually grasp a rattle and shake it in a controlled way. At this stage he is quite likely to bang his head with it or poke it in his eye. However, you can string rattles and other brightly colored objects across the crib so that he can look at and reach out for them while lying on his back. He will watch them with interest.

A baby of this age is probably too young to cuddle soft toys although he may respond to those that squeak or rattle. He will probably enjoy looking at colorful pictures though, so you can try tucking some cards between the mattress and the side of his crib or stroller.

week 14

month	*date*

MON

_____

TUES

_____

WED

_____

THURS

_____

FRI

_____

SAT

_____

SUN

LEARNING TO ROLL

Your baby may start to roll from her back to her side at this time, and it is doubly important that you do not leave her, even for a moment, lying down on the changing table or on the bed.

When lying on her tummy, she may make 'swimming' movements with her arms and legs. And if you hold her upright on your knee, she will enjoy 'bouncing' and taking some of her weight on her legs.

Once your baby can roll over, it won't matter which way you put her down at night. You may lie her on her back and later find her on her tummy. Occasionally, though, a baby who has learned to roll may get stuck, and wake up crying. Don't wedge a blanket down the side of the crib to prevent her rolling over. She could suffocate.

Some babies become mobile through rolling over and over long before they learn to crawl. You will need to adopt some of the safety measures in Weeks 15 and 30, as a rolling baby can move a surprising distance in a short space of time. In particular, beware of your baby rolling towards dangerous objects such as a fire or ironing board.

Once your baby has learned to roll over you may need to alter some habits such as changing her diaper on a changing table.

*n*OTES

_____

*L*EAVING BABY AT HOME

*Y*ou should feel ready to start going out and doing some of the things you did before she was born, even if it is only a trip to the cinema or a restaurant in the evening, or to have your hair cut during the day. The first time you leave your baby and go out can be rather alarming – many mothers feel as if they have inadvertently left something behind!

See Week 36 for Time to Yourself

The baby's feed

If you are breast-feeding, you can express milk to leave for your baby in a bottle. Expressed breast-milk will keep in a sterile container in the refrigerator for forty-eight hours or if you can't express enough at once, you can freeze a little at a time for a few days before you go out and store it in the freezer. It is quite safe to add a little to already frozen milk kept in the freezer.

You can buy or rent breast pumps if you cannot manage the technique of expressing by hand; these need to be carefully sterilized like all other feeding equipment. Some mothers find that they cannot 'let down' their milk when using a pump; it can help to use a pump to express from one side while the baby is feeding at the other breast. Expressed breast-milk often looks thin and watery or may even separate on standing; this doesn't mean that it has gone bad, and the milk will return to normal consistency when it is warmed up.

If you are bottle-feeding, prepare a bottle in advance for the baby-sitter or your partner to give to your baby.

Fathers

It can be hard for the father to involve himself very much with the baby in the early weeks, especially if you are breast-feeding. But it will help the father make a firm relationship with the baby if he is sometimes left in sole charge, while you spend an evening out with friends.

Even if you are breast-feeding, it may be a good idea to express milk so that the father can give a bottle at night once in a while – although you have to be able to sleep through the baby's crying while he warms the bottle if this is to be worthwhile.

ABOUT BABY-SITTERS

It is of course important that you leave your baby with someone that you know and trust, and preferably someone familiar to the baby as well.

Make sure the baby-sitter knows how to warm and give a bottle. Remind her, for example, to loosen the top of the bottle to let air in and milk out! If she has not done it before, show her how to change a diaper too. Describe what you usually do when the baby wakes, and if she has any particular routine. It's a good idea to leave everything ready for the baby-sitter – a change of clothes laid out, a diaper already folded – in the place where it will be needed.

Always leave a number where you can be contacted in an emergency or the number of another mother who is a neighbor if the sitter is young and inexperienced.

week 15

month   date

MON

TUES

7/18 1:15pm rolled back to front

WED

7/19 rolled back to front front to back across a blanket

THURS

FRI

SAT

SUN

*n*OTES

Never leave within your baby's reach small objects which he could swallow, like coins, pins, buttons, small pieces of Lego or other pieces from older children's toys. Do not give him anything sharp or too heavy to use as a rattle as he is likely to hit himself with it.

Never leave your baby unattended on a raised surface as he can easily roll over and fall off.

If you have him on your lap at mealtimes, be careful that he does not suddenly reach out and grab at bowls or mugs of hot liquid standing on the table.

If you have a pet, don't leave your baby unattended near the animal, who could try and sleep on his face or bite or scratch if the baby makes an unintended swipe.

Mugs and cups of hot liquid are among the commonest causes of burns and scalds to young children.

BABY IN THE DAYTIME

As your baby approaches four months the range of things he can handle increases. At this age lying him on a mat on the floor, with rattles and other safe objects, can provide fairly long periods of contented play. He may enjoy lying on his tummy and lifting himself up on his hands to reach out for any toys or objects close by. He may even be able to move his body a little by rolling over.

A baby of this age may be old enough for a playpen. Although he is nowhere near mobile, a playpen provides a place in which his toys can be kept, and can even be a safe place to snuggle down if he is sleepy. You can hang interesting objects from the bars of a playpen or safety gate for the baby to swipe at. If there are other children or adults around, you won't have to worry about them stepping on the baby or about pets possibly bothering him. It also helps to get a baby used to a playpen now, or he may never accept the idea of it. An easily cleaned safety mat inside the playpen can be tied to the bars to protect the baby and your floorcovering.

An activity center is a good investment at this age; it can be fixed to the bars of the crib or playpen. It will provide entertainment for months to come. Other popular toys for this stage are weighted objects which can be pushed over so they bounce back, and soft toys which squeak or make a sound. However, a baby of this age is happy to be 'entertained' without toys: he will get a lot of pleasure from walks, from bathtime games such as trickling water on his tummy and other gentle games (see Week 18). He may also enjoy hearing music on the radio. If you don't want to spend a lot of money on toys, you can make your own rattles, mobiles and cloth blocks from household materials.

Even if your baby is happy to spend some of his time playing with toys, remember that you are still his main source of pleasure and security so try to make time to talk to him and demonstrate how things work. You can always chat and sing to him as you work.

By four months it is safer for the baby to begin sleeping in a crib if he has been in a bassinet or cradle so far. You can put soft toys in the crib for your baby to play with on going to bed and waking, but make sure they do not have anything that the baby could swallow.

See Week 11 for Choosing a Crib

week 16

month   date

MON

TUES

WED

THURS

FRI
7/27 - ate cereal
from a spoon

SAT

SUN

*n*OTES

Your baby is probably ready for solid foods when she is four months old and:
- She starts to drool – until she starts to make a lot of saliva she may find solids hard to cope with.
- She starts to chew on toys and other things.
- She starts to put her fingers and other objects in her mouth.
- She shows less need or desire to suck for its own sake.
- She appears dissatisfied after a feeding or starts demanding extra feedings in twenty-four hours.
- She starts waking for a feeding in the night after having been sleeping through. Ask your doctor if you are unsure whether to increase the baby's milk or to start her on solids.

Never add salt to baby food that you are preparing. This can be harmful as the baby's kidneys are unable to cope with too much salt in their diet. Too much sugar can also be harmful, as well as encouraging a 'sweet tooth'. On the whole, babies who are not given any sweet things will not refuse wholesome, flavorful foods.

Don't forget It is time for your baby's second DTP, polio, and HIB shots.

ƒIRST SOLIDS

A young baby is unable to digest solid foods before at least three months and the earlier you give other foods, the more likely she is to develop an allergy to them. However, there will come a time when your baby starts to demand more food, and it will be obvious that milk alone seems not to satisify her.

Start off with small quantities and don't give your baby too many new foods at a time – if one food seems to upset her, you will immediately know which it is. At this stage the foods are really 'tastes' rather than meals, and you may have more success in giving them if you offer them when the baby is not too hungry. Some mothers sandwich first solids in the middle of a breast- or bottle-feeding; others find it easier to give a 'snack' between meals.

If your baby doesn't take to solids at first, don't despair; she doesn't really need them yet. Just keep offering them and sooner or later she will get the idea. If she appears to spit them out, this may be her attempts at swallowing.

You may find trying to prepare and feed small amounts both frustrating and time-consuming, especially if most of the food ends up on the baby's clothes! If you have a freezer, sterilize a plastic ice tray and fill it with cubes of puréed food – you then only have to pop one or two out when needed. Prepared baby foods seem easy at this stage, but if your baby gets used to tasting at least some home-prepared foods from the beginning, this may prevent her from becoming a fussy eater later on.

If the food you use is cooked and freshly prepared, you do not have to sterilize the bowl, spoon and grater – they should be clean of course, and you can rinse them in boiling water before using them. If food is to be stored in the refrigerator for up to forty-eight hours, you should sterilize the container.

See Week 19 for Baby's Meals

It is important to remember that the baby is only used to swallowing liquids so make the first foods as soft as possible and let her suck them off the spoon.

WHAT TO GIVE

The best first solids are gluten-free cereals, such as rice, or fruit purées. Rice needs to be ground and cooked and mixed with the milk you are giving your baby, whether this is expressed breast-milk or formula. You can use boiled, cooled water.

Fruit should be cooked and puréed, except for banana, which needs to be ripe and mashed till liquid. You can also give her purées of cooked vegetables such as carrots, potatoes and cauliflower, although some breast-fed babies are disappointed that the last two are not sweet.

week 17

month   *date*

MON

TUES
- 2nd set of shots
7/31 weighs 16 lbs 13 oz
and is 26 1/2 in long
WED started baby food - carrots - loved it

THURS

FRI

SAT

SUN

*n*OTES

FIRST SOUNDS

By three months most babies will be having limited 'conversations' with their mothers. The baby will watch his mother's face and make cooing sounds, and he will often try to imitate her sounds. He will become more adventurous once he gets used to the sound of his own voice.

A little later he may start to look around for the source of a sound. He may look at something he can see, rather than what made the sound. A baby of this age will 'talk' most when spoken to by a familiar person, although some babies will babble away to toys or even the television. The sounds he makes usually indicate contentment and may lead to real laughter when he is particularly amused by some activity.

You will get hours of pleasure from your first conversations with your baby.

*M*EETING OTHER MOTHERS

*I*f you are at home on your own with the baby there are going to be times when you feel at a loss for what to do. Perhaps the baby is unusually wakeful or irritable one day and you are unable to meet his demands. At such times it is a great help if you can go out and meet someone or do something enjoyable together.

Having a young child will often help you to meet fellow mothers as well as neighbors, including those without children. It is a good idea to arrange to take your babies for a walk together sometimes, so that you can enjoy an adult conversation while the babies are being entertained by strolling. You might meet other women at the doctor's office.

If you were working before the baby was born, you may hardly have met any of your neighbors and other people in your area. They may stop to chat and admire the baby when you are out for a walk – take the opportunity to talk to them and perhaps invite them in for a cup of coffee. Once you know your neighbors, you may find that they can help out in emergencies – perhaps minding the baby for a short time while you run out to the pharmacy on a rainy evening. Equally, you might be able to help them out, too, perhaps doing some shopping for an elderly neighbor while doing your own.

If you are not returning to work, there may be other activities going on in the neighborhood in which you could become involved. The local school district may run evening adult education classes. Some of them may even provide child-care. Or you may be able to take an evening exercise class where you will meet other people in your area.

See Week 49 for Meeting other children

SUPPORT GROUPS

- New parent groups are always starting up; check the ads in your community newspaper, at the local Y, your local school board.
- There may be a family resource or mothers' center in your area. These are usually set up and run by parents and are designed to meet the social and parenting needs of new mothers and fathers. Contact the National Association of Mothers' Centers, MELD (Minnesota Early Learning Design), or The Family Resource Coalition (see Useful Addresses, p. 110).
- The La Leche League runs breast-feeding support groups, which are generally groups of mothers who meet on a regular basis. Contact a local chapter of La Leche League International (see Useful Addresses, p. 110).

You could set up a regular morning or afternoon a week for new mothers to meet for coffee. Your prepared-childbirth instructor or your pediatrician can probably put you in touch with new parents.

week 18

month _____ *date* _____

MON
_____

TUES
~~Th. debslka.~~
_____

WED
_____

THURS
_____

FRI
_____

SAT
_____

SUN
_____

*n*OTES

WEANING FROM BREAST TO BOTTLE

Many mothers find the emotional rewards of breast-feeding increase as their baby gets older. Other mothers, however, feel that breast-feeding is less important once solid foods are introduced. If you decide to change to bottle-feeding, you must not feel guilty; you have given your baby an excellent start.

The best way to stop is gradually. Replace one breast-feeding every other day or so with a bottle, so that your milk gradually decreases and you do not feel too uncomfortable. Drop a feeding when you have less milk and the baby needs less comfort – bedtime feedings may be the last to go.

Some babies will reject the bottle at first: if so, continue to offer it at the same time over a period of days. Try leaving the baby longer so that she is more hungry. Some babies become angry with this treatment and may turn against the bottle; try not to make it a battle between you.

Babies at this age may take to the bottle readily.

*g*AMES TO PLAY

*t*here are several simple exercises which you can do with a baby of this age. Many babies enjoy standing on the floor and bouncing on their legs, testing out taking their weight, but they need to be held firmly while you bounce them. They will also like bouncing games on your knee. Most babies also enjoy being lifted up into the air and returned to safety.

Playing with your baby in this way helps her to exercise muscles she cannot use unaided, as well as providing pleasurable entertainment for you both.

By the time the baby is four to five months old, she is not only more robust but also very responsive. Many parents find physical play with babies of this age very rewarding as the baby obviously derives great pleasure from it.

GAMES AND EXERCISES FOR YOUR BABY

- Lie on your back on the floor with your knees raised and the baby sitting on your stomach, resting against your knees. Hold her hands and, as you sit up, lower her so that you are facing each other – then say 'boo'. Repeat, pulling her up as you lie down.
- Lie on your back and rest your baby on the lower part of your legs. Bring your knees up so that the baby 'takes off' and lift her arms up into the air.

- Sit your baby facing you on your lap, and hold her hands. Say: 'This is the way the lady rides, trit-trot, trit-trot, trit-trot' (jogging very gently). 'This is the way the gentleman rides, a-gallop, a-gallop, a-gallop' (jogging with alternate legs). 'This is the way the farmer rides, hobbledy-hoy, hobbledy-hoy' (uneven jiggling like a limping horse) '– and down into a ditch!' (dropping her gently).
- Bounce your baby on your knee to the tune of 'All

around the mulberry bush the monkey chased the weasel, the monkey said it was all in fun, pop goes the weasel!'
- Sit on the floor with your legs stretched out and the baby lying looking up at you, her head towards your toes. Hold her hands and pull her up towards you as you lean back, and lower her as you rock forward, singing: 'Row, row, row your boat, gently down the stream, merrily, merrily, merrily, merrily, life is but a dream.'

week 19

MON

TUES

WED

THURS

FRI

SAT

SUN

CRYING AND COMFORTING

As your baby gets older you will realize the reason for his crying. He will generally cry from hunger only before established feeding times, or from tiredness at the times of day when he usually sleeps. You will know whether he is crying from frustration, or boredom, or because he wants you to pick him up. If your baby cries a lot more than usual you will have to assume that he is ill or is suffering from some discomfort such as teething.

However, your baby's pattern may change; he may cry when you put him down for his morning nap because he is not ready to sleep. When he is acquiring a new skill that uses a lot of energy, he may be more tired than usual and need a little *more* sleep.

As he grows, he will need more stimulation and he may become bored if the toys and distractions he is given do not meet his new need to grasp, hold, and exercise.

*n*OTES

*a*s your baby becomes used to first solids on a spoon and the tastes of two or three different foods, you can start to build up these tastes into proper meals. It is best to proceed quite slowly, but to start giving the baby more at one particular meal – usually either lunch or dinner, whichever is most convenient for you. The best foods are still cereals and puréed fruits and vegetables, but you can try adding a little unsalted gravy or sieved meat. It is best to steer clear of eggs, cheese and strawberries for a while yet because some babies are allergic to them or find them indigestible.

Introduce new foods one at a time so that you can be sure what it is if anything upsets your baby. Remember that his digestive system is still geared to a milk diet and that new foods may cause a slight digestive upset. A baby of this age won't be able to digest everything he's given.

At this age you should avoid giving your baby any adult convenience foods, or any salt. A baby's kidneys are not mature enough for him to handle salt in any quantity. Foods containing a lot of salt or sugar will also make your baby thirsty; if he fills up with juice or other drinks he may not have room for the milk he needs. However, packages and jars of ready-made baby foods have their place and can be quick and convenient (see below).

Save yourself time by cooking a little extra when preparing your own meals; leave out the spices and flavorings and add salt or sugar to your meal later. You can also freeze small portions of baby food in yogurt containers or plastic ice trays in the freezer, or keep them for up to two days in the refrigerator.

It would be worth investing in a blender or food processor at this stage; it will be in constant use for months.

See Week 22 for Teething

CONVENIENCE BABY FOODS

Since many jars and boxes of ready-made baby foods have the same bland taste and texture, it is worth getting your baby used to the taste of homemade foods. Always look carefully at the ingredients on boxes and jars. For example, you might want to avoid cow's milk products and find that a prepackaged meal contains large quantities of milk. Look for labels that indicate no added sugar on packages of biscuits and cereals as well as on jars of baby food. Desserts may contain sugar, and many convenience foods have added starch and protein. Homemade foods with no added starch or sugar are best for a plump baby.

Convenience foods do have their place, however, especially when away from home. It might be more valuable to spend half an hour playing with your baby than leaving him to cry while you boil up and purée carrots or grate some meat.

week 20

month   *date*

MON

TUES

WED
8/22 26 in long
      18 lbs. 4 oz.

THURS

FRI

SAT

SUN

*n*OTES

FEELING HER FEET

Around this time your baby may discover her feet and enjoy playing with them whenever she gets the opportunity, especially in the bath or while having her diaper changed. She will enjoy being on the floor on a rug with her feet uncovered.

She will like to stand upright, supported by you, and take her weight on her legs. At first she will probably bounce with both legs together, but then she will learn to hop and dance, taking the weight on one foot and then the other.

If you support your baby under the armpits, she will enjoy the sensation of taking her weight on her feet.

Once your baby is introduced to a mixed diet, her bowel movements change in consistency; they smell different too and in some cases diaper rash may result. Some babies become a little constipated when starting solids, while others have loose and frequent bowel movements. The baby's digestive system needs time to adjust to new foods and the bacteria present in the baby's intestine tend to change. Mothers who have so far breast-fed may find diaper rash occurs when they introduce formula milk.

The most common form of diaper rash is caused by bacteria in the baby's bowel movements attacking substances in the baby's urine, to produce ammonia. This powerful alkali may smell very strong and it will certainly inflame her skin. If the skin gets sore and broken, it can be difficult to cure, so prompt action is necessary as soon as the diaper rash starts.

Thrush is another cause of persistent diaper rash. This is a fungus which also lives in the baby's intestine and which causes a characteristic raised red rash, which may resist all treatment. It is possible to see the fungus as a white substance on the skin, but you may mistake it for zinc and castor oil cream. If your baby has thrush, a doctor will prescribe an antifungal medicine to clear it up quickly.

Some babies have very sensitive skin and may be allergic to the washing powder or fabric conditioner you are using, or to diaper softeners – or even to the substances used to perfume disposable diapers. If you think this could be the cause, try using diaper liners and changing the brand of disposable diapers, or change your clothes detergent to a milder one.

Leave your baby to kick without a diaper to allow the air to get to her skin. Remember not to leave her unattended on a raised changing mat – put the mat on the floor where you can watch her.

PREVENTING DIAPER RASH

It helps to change the baby's diaper frequently. If you can let her kick for a while without a diaper on, perhaps on a towel or a cloth diaper on a waterproof mat, that will also help. (The baby's skin can stick to a plastic mat, especially on hot days.) The bacteria which cause the problem do not survive well if exposed to air.

Always wash your baby's bottom well and dry it carefully when you change a diaper, to remove bacteria from her skin. Then apply a good barrier cream, such as zinc and castor oil or petroleum jelly.

week 21

month   _date_

MON

TUES

WED

THURS

FRI

SAT

SUN

_n_OTES

ROUGH AND TUMBLE GAMES

Below are some ideas for more physical 'games' to play with your baby. Some babies do not enjoy these rougher games, however, and find the sensation of being thrown in the air or suddenly 'dropped' very alarming. If this is the case, find something gentler to play with your baby.

Aeroplanes _Hold the baby around his chest and 'fly' him around the room, swooping down and then up into the air._

Playing football _Rest the baby on your knee, take his legs and mimic running with them, before pretending to kick a ball into a goal; you could give a running football commentary as you do it!_

ƒATHERS

See Week 18
for Games to
Play

*a*t around this stage the baby may start to become more interesting to his father. Some fathers find tiny babies alarming, and do not feel confident in handling them. But as the baby becomes bigger and more robust, and begins to interact more with people, the father may, once the baby responds to him, discover he has a part to play.

At this same age many babies start to show an interest in familiar people other than their mother and to react to them as individuals. The particular characteristics of his father may be endlessly interesting for the baby – his more rugged features and his different voice.

If your partner takes the baby around with him while he is doing household chores from time to time, this will encourage the baby to think of his father as another loving person. If you are thinking of returning to work in the near future, it is even more important for the father to involve himself in the baby's care. Not only can he help when you are not there, but the baby will be accustomed to being handled by someone other than his mother by the time childcare arrangements begin.

SHARING THE ROUTINE

It helps to build a strong relationship if the father develops a habit of doing something regularly with the baby. If your partner goes off to work early and the baby is an early riser, this can be a good time for him to get the baby up, perhaps amuse him while shaving or getting breakfast – and give you an extra half-hour in bed or some time to have a bath in peace.

Alternatively, the father may like to give his baby a bath at the end of the day. Fathers can involve themselves with their baby in other everyday ways too, such as changing diapers and clothes,

getting him ready to go out, or giving the baby some of his solid food. This will help the baby to realize that food and comfort come from other people too.

This kind of support is all the more welcome when your partner doesn't wait to be asked to do things. It can be a great help to feel that the responsibility for the child is being understood and shared. A father who sometimes offers to take the baby off your hands, or who notices the baby needs changing before it has to be pointed out to him, will be taking away some of this pressure.

Building a bridge
It is important that every time the baby cries the father doesn't automatically hand him over to you. This would only reinforce the message that mother is the only source of comfort and will make it more difficult for the baby to form a relationship with, and trust, other adults. The father plays an important role in providing a bridge between the baby and you and the outside world. The closer and more involved he becomes, the easier the baby's adjustment to the changes will be. Everyone will benefit if the parenting is shared.

week 22

month　　　　*date*

MON
8/3　rolled back
　　　to front

TUES

WED

THURS

FRI

SAT

SUN

*n*OTES

LOOKING AFTER TEETH

When your baby has several teeth, you can put a little toothpaste on your finger and rub them gently. An older baby will enjoy chewing on a toothbrush but is unlikely to do any effective cleaning.

Help her to grow strong teeth by giving fluoride drops – check with your doctor as to the level of fluoride in the local water supply and what dosage you should give, if any. If you are regularly rubbing a fluoride toothpaste on her teeth, be careful not to let her swallow toothpaste as she could be getting too much fluoride.

The best way to ensure healthy teeth is to avoid giving your child too many sweet things. It is particularly important not to give her sweet drinks in a bottle as the constant bathing of the teeth in sweet liquids can cause severe damage to growing teeth.

*t*EETHING

abies vary considerably in the age at which they cut their teeth, though they generally come through in the same order. Most babies cut their first teeth around five to seven months, though it is possible to have a first tooth as early as three months or as late as a year.

Teething is often blamed for many of the baby's troubles in the first year. While teething may cause some fretting, drooling and frantic biting, it is unlikely to be the cause of more serious symptoms. If a baby is ill she should be taken to the doctor, and if she is crying or fretful you should look for some other cause such as boredom, thirst or a cold.

Remember, too, that your baby drools because she does not know how to swallow the saliva that is constantly being produced to clean and lubricate her mouth. At some time near the beginning of the second year she will learn to swallow this. Some babies drool so much that their clothes are always wet as are the sheets on her crib and carriage. You can use a bib while she is awake and put something absorbent under her head while she sleeps. It is dangerous to let a baby sleep with a bib tied round her neck.

See Week 10 for Baby's First Illness

See Week 48 for Healthy Teeth

TEETHERS

If your baby appears in discomfort over teething, simply massaging her gums with your little finger may provide comfort. You can also help her by giving her hard things to bite or chew on, such as crusts. Never leave her alone with these because of the danger of choking.

Special teething rattles can be bought or teething devices with a gel inside them which can be cooled in the refrigerator. (Never use such a teething ring direct from the freezer as it will be so cold it could burn the baby's mouth.)

Teething gels, available at pharmacies, can be rubbed on the baby's gums to anesthetize them slightly; provided you do not use them too often, they are unlikely to cause any harm. Don't get into the habit of regularly giving your baby acetaminophen syrup or other commercial painkillers.

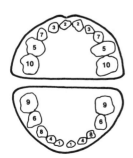

The first teeth to come through are usually the front incisors, or the two middle teeth of the lower jaw, then the upper incisors. These are followed by the lower first molars and then the upper first molars at around twelve to fourteen months. The lower and upper canines – the sharp 'eye teeth' – are cut at about eighteen months.

week 23

MON

TUES

WED

THURS

FRI

SAT

SUN

*n*OTES

HAND-EYE COORDINATION

Your baby is learning to focus and will soon be able to assess the distance between his hand and a particular object and judge how far he has to reach. Instead of swiping at an object with a clenched fist, he will open his hands and wrap them around it.

He may bring the toy or object in his hand up to his mouth to explore it further, or at least nearer to his face so that he can study it more closely. He may try shaking it and, quite soon, will be able to feel it with both hands.

Objects which make a noise are particularly good for developing your baby's hand-eye coordination. He will learn that what he does with his hands can create a sound as well as making an object move where he wants it.

Don't forget At least once a day, do something just for you.

*l*ooking after a baby is hard work, so it is important that you keep fit and healthy. You have had a lot taken out of you in the last year and if you are still feeling less fit than before you had the baby, or if you are overweight, start thinking about what you can do to change this.

Most crucial of all is your diet: make sure that you are eating well. If you are rushing around, you may not have time to fix proper meals for yourself but fill up on snacks instead. Try to sit down at lunchtime when you feed your baby and eat something satisfying, even if it is only a simple meal like soup and a roll of wholewheat bread, or a sandwich made with wholewheat bread, cheese, peanut butter or meat and salad. Eat fruit rather than sweets and increase your milk intake – if you don't like drinking milk, try taking it in another more palatable form for you such as yogurt or low-fat cheeses.

If you can find the time, start doing some regular exercise. Try to turn your exercises into a game that you and the baby can play together – he may even be amused simply to watch you. If you find this hard on your own, join a local exercise class.

Swimming is excellent all-round exercise; some swimming pools have special sessions for mothers and babies and, if you go with a friend, one of you can mind the babies while the other gets some actual swimming done.

BACK STRENGTHENING
Lie face downwards with your forehead resting on your hands. Lift one leg behind you from the hip, keeping it straight. Lift it as high as you can, without bending the knee or turning your body. Lower it again and relax. Lift the other leg and relax. Continue the exercise several times.

FIRMING YOUR BREASTS
Stand or sit upright. Grasp your wrists with alternate hands, and lift both arms up until elbows, shoulders and wrists are level; hold this position. Grip really hard, and try to push your wrists towards your elbows. Push and relax several times.

TRIMMING THE WAISTLINE
Lie on your back with arms outstretched and bent knees together. Keeping your feet and shoulders still, and twisting from your waist, swing both knees over to touch the floor or bed on the left, while your right hip points towards the ceiling. Then swing your knees over to the right, so your left hip turns towards the ceiling. Repeat several times.

week 24

month	date

MON

TUES

WED

THURS

FRI

SAT

SUN

LEARNING TO SIT

By about four months your baby will be able to sit if you support her. By the age of six months she may be able to sit up by herself for a few seconds. Sit her on the floor propped up with cushions which will soften her landing when she flops.

Many babies can sit alone by about seven months, though they are unsteady. Their backs will be rounded and they may use their arms to support themselves.

At this stage it is rather unkind to sit your baby up surrounded by toys as the moment she lifts a hand off the ground she is bound to fall over. Try sitting with her to give her support and encouragement.

At first your baby's back will be very rounded and her head will pull her forward, so you will need to support her in a sitting position.

Once your baby can sit alone for short periods, you can support her with cushions. Cushions on the floor will prevent her from hurting herself when she falls over.

*n*OTES

52

bABY'S CHANGING DIET

*a*s your baby approaches six months she will be eating more solid food and cutting down on the amount of milk she needs in compensation. By now she may be eating three small meals a day and you can try cutting out the lunchtime breast- or bottle-feeding. Give water or baby fruit juice – either in a bottle or in a trainer cup.

If you want your baby to eat a wide range of foods, it is important that you try to cut down on the amount of milk she drinks and offer a broad variety of foods to get her used to different tastes and textures. You can offer breast- or bottle-feedings after a meal – you should find she drinks less naturally. Some babies, however, seem to prefer sucking on the breast or bottle to taking solid foods and you may have to go more slowly.

But a baby who is taking five full bottles a day is not going to have room for solid foods – and if she does eat them, she is likely to get fat.

At this stage it is also important that your baby gets plenty to drink as she will no longer be getting all the fluids she needs from milk. Offer plain boiled and cooled water – though some babies, used to sweet breast-milk or formula, find this a bit of an insult. If so, use diluted baby fruit juice – preferably unsweetened mixed with boiled water – and try giving it in a trainer cup.

By six months your baby may be ready to take her meals in a highchair. Always stay with your baby – you will need to feed her at first and if she is chewing on a rusk or finger food you should be at hand in case she chokes or tries to climb out.

Give your baby a trainer cup with milk or diluted juice in it. Even if she doesn't drink from it give her an unbreakable cup with handles which she can play with so that she gets used to the cup at mealtimes. Eventually she will get the idea of what it is for.

SAMPLE MENU

Early morning Breast/bottle-feeding.
Breakfast Cereal (warm, sugar-free baby cereal) then breast/bottle-feeding.

Lunch Puréed meat or fish and vegetables, or a jar meal, followed by pureed fruit.
Supper/Late afternoon Puréed fruit or mashed banana with

cereal, followed by breast/bottle-feeding. You could mix the fruit with natural yogurt once your baby is six months old.
Bedtime Breast/bottle-feeding.

week 25

month   date

MON

TUES

WED

THURS

0/27- can sit up streight for a little bit w/o help

FRI

SAT

SUN

SOCIAL BEHAVIOR

Your baby will now recognize other familiar faces as well as your own and may greet them with pleasure. But he may also begin to show fear of strange people, especially if they try to be too familiar, picking him up suddenly or making a fuss over him. Some babies show pronounced 'stranger anxiety' by crying and appearing distressed if an unfamiliar person picks them up.

Babies of this age are unlikely to intereact much with babies or other children they don't know well, though you may notice your baby plays quietly for longer if another baby is with him, and he may watch the antics of older children with pleasure as long as they are not too noisy.

Don't forget Continue with your pelvic floor exercises (see Week 6).

Don't forget Continue with your pelvic floor exercises (see Week 6).

*n*OTES

RETURNING TO WORK?

You will probably have to decide sometime this year whether or not you will be returning to work. Under the new Family and Medical Leave Act, you may take up to 12 weeks off, without pay, to give birth or to care for a newborn or newly adopted or foster child – if your employer has more than 50 employees within a 75-mile radius and you have worked for the employer for at least 12 months (but not necessarily consecutively). However, you must give your employer at least 30 days notice. For more information, you can call a hotline operated by '9 to 5' (1-800-522-0925).

If your maternity leave is up and you decide to resume working, it may help to work a shorter work week or leave early the first week or two. An ideal solution is to try to dovetail your work schedule with your partner's, so that one of you can be at home in the early months. Before you return to work be sure to have a trial day when you leave your baby in the care of the baby-sitter or day care provider.

CHOICE OF CHILDCARE

Few companies provide on-site day care, although they may offer subsidies at privately-run day care centers in the area. To find out what's available in your community ask parents you know who have young children, your doctor, a child-care referral agency (or the National Association of Childcare Resources – see Useful Addresses, p. 110), churches or synagogues, and schools. Common options include:

Family day care
Generally more economical than hiring an au pair or a caregiver to come to your home is finding another parent who cares for children in her home. This is referred to as 'family day care'. Not all states require family-day-care homes to be licensed; to find out about regulations in your state, call its childcare licensing office or resource-and-referral agency. It's best when the family-day-care provider limits the number of children she cares for to no more than three children under the age of three, including her own. Be sure to arrange a visit to the home – allow at least 90 minutes and bring your child. Observe how the caregiver interacts with the children, if she shows common sense, displays affection towards the children, and is prepared for emergencies. Ask for the names of parents you can call as references.

Preschool or day care centers
Some communities have public day care centers and parents pay on a sliding scale. Most common are private day care centers operated on a for-profit or non-profit basis; they may be in churches, synagogues, colleges or universities. For-profit day care centers are often called 'learning centers'. Each option needs to be carefully investigated.

MAKING THE DECISION

Most mothers feel guilty to some extent about leaving their child to go to work, and some may be conscious of the disapproval of either friends or relatives. It is worth thinking carefully about your own views and feelings. If you really think working isn't a good idea, you will probably find the guilt and stress very difficult to deal with, especially if other people put pressure on you. If your arrangements are suitable, there is no need to feel guilty.

However, you may decide that you have to work for financial reasons, or you may feel that working enables you to afford some of the extras that make life a little easier for you and your children, or that you want to pursue your career. Many mothers, particularly those who are able to work part-time, feel that they get more out of their children and enjoy the time they are together much more because they also have a break from them.

week 26

month   date

MON
16

TUES

WED

THURS

FRI

SAT

SUN

*n*OTES

SIX-MONTH MILESTONES

By six months your baby may want to feed herself by grabbing the spoon or picking up bits of food in her fingers.

She is probably able to sit for a few seconds on her own, or for longer propped up with cushions, and can roll from her stomach to her back and possibly vice versa. She may make crawling movements, though she is unlikely to make any real progress at this age.

She can reach accurately for objects within her reach and pick them up using her whole hand. She can also pick up an object with both hands, and will drop what she is holding if you offer something else.

Your baby will by now recognize a number of familiar faces and show particular pleasure in her mother and father. She may treat your body as if it is her own, poking fingers in your mouth and nose, while showing more respect for less familiar faces.

Don't forget It is time for your baby's 3rd DTP, HIB, and Hepatitus B shots.

*e*ATING AND SLEEPING

by the six-month stage your baby should have a fairly fixed routine of meals, nap times and bedtime. Up to now, she may have fitted in round your changing day. Now it becomes more important to keep the baby to a regular routine if you are to avoid problems.

Most babies of this age will need two naps a day: one in the morning and one in the afternoon. The length of her naps will depend on how much sleep she needs overall and on the time she goes to bed in the evening.

If your baby is wakeful, try to extend her 'nap' times by putting toys in the crib for her to play with on waking, or before she settles herself for a nap. Even if the baby doesn't sleep, it can refresh you both if she goes in her crib to play quietly while you get on with other things or put your feet up for twenty minutes or so. If she gets into the habit of playing in her crib at set times, she may accept this for quite long periods.

Mealtimes should be regular by now, and will fit around the baby's preferred nap times. For example, if your baby sleeps late in the morning, from 11.30 a.m.-1 p.m., she may not have her lunch until 1.30 p.m. and supper not until 6 p.m. Another baby might nap from 9.30 a.m.-11 a.m. and be ready for lunch at midday; she may not be able to last later than 4.30 p.m. for supper and may then want something extra before finally going to bed.

If your baby wakes later, she may join the family in their breakfast, but an early riser may need her breakfast sooner, unless her early morning breast- or bottle-feeding is enough to keep her going until you are ready to eat.

See Week 40 for Coping with Sleep Problems

BREAKING THE NIGHT WAKING HABIT

Your six-month-old baby may still be waking at night. If you are still giving breast- or bottle-feedings at night, try to cut this out. The baby does not need the extra nourishment if she is eating well during the day, and giving her milk may stimulate her digestion, making sleep more difficult. Try offering water or diluted baby fruit juice in a training cup instead.

When she wakes, gradually give her less and less attention. Don't talk to her and don't put the light on; just check that all is well, offer a drink if you think she might be thirsty, then put her back in her crib and leave her. Let her cry a little, and if the crying persists go back and settle her again in the same way, until she goes back to sleep. If you are still breast-feeding, it may be better if your partner goes to her. Many parents steel themselves for a hard time and discover, to their surprise, that their baby settles down after a few nights.

week27

month   date

MON
10/8 1st tooth is budding on bottom right!

TUES

WED

THURS

FRI

SAT

SUN

NOTES

THE DOCTOR'S EXAMINATION

Help the doctor to examine your baby by holding him gently but firmly on your lap. When visiting the doctor, remember to dress him in clothes which come off easily.

For a throat examination, cradle the baby's head in your arm and hold his hands down so that he cannot try to push the doctor's hands away. Talk reassuringly.

So that the doctor can examine your baby's ears, hold him firmly on your lap. Turn him for the other ear to be checked.

COMMON ILLNESSES

babies and small children are likely to catch colds and other minor illnesses simply because they have built up little resistance to them, having not been exposed to them before. While a baby is breast-fed, the mother passes on her immunity to a range of illnesses, but this gradually wears off after the baby is weaned. Towards the end of the first year, and throughout his second year, your baby may become ill with something other than a cold.

Coughs and colds

Many babies have a high temperature at the beginning of an ordinary cold, and a baby with an illness such as German measles or roseola can run a very high fever. If your baby has a raised temperature, keep him cool – take blankets off his crib, for example, and if he is really hot sponge him down with cool water. Acetaminophen syrup will bring down a temperature as well as relieving pain. If the temperature stays high, consult your doctor.

Coughs and colds sometimes lead to other infections of the throat, ear or lungs, because thick mucus provides an ideal breeding ground for bacteria. A secondary infection may result in another sudden rise in temperature after the baby had seemed much better. A baby with a sore throat will be restless and may refuse food or drink, or may be sick. An ear infection can cause severe pain and the baby may tug or pull his ear.

Childhood diseases

Measles, chicken pox, mumps, German measles, roseola and whooping cough are the most common childhood diseases. You can protect your baby against whooping cough from two months and against measles at around thirteen months. A vaccine for mumps and German measles (rubella) is given with the measles vaccine.

German measles and roseola are usually mild, especially in young babies. They rarely last long and need no special treatment. Chicken pox can be mild or quite severe and you should try to prevent your baby scratching or the spots can become infected. Measles can take quite a severe form and is sometimes followed by ear or lung infections, so the baby should be nursed carefully. Always see your doctor to confirm that your child has any of these illnesses; he or she can help make the correct diagnosis and offer advice.

Nursing your child

If your baby is ill, you will have to drop everything else and dedicate yourself to looking after him. Many ill babies require a great deal of comforting and may need to be carried around all the time. A baby with a fever will often be very drowsy but sleep only for short periods before waking in obvious pain and crying again.

Offer frequent drinks of water or diluted juice. Offer food if he will take it, but don't press food on an ill baby who doesn't want it; this may make him sick. Some babies with a temperature produce very strong urine which stings them, and others may have diarrhea, so change diapers frequently and use a protective cream to prevent diaper rash.

An ill baby usually means broken nights, so go to bed early yourself and get as much rest as you can. You could sleep in a spare bed next to the crib to reduce the disruption and to reassure the baby.

See Week 10 for Baby's First Illness

See Week 8 for First Immunizations

GIVING MEDICINE

Many medicines are extremely sweet and most babies will like taking them; offer medicine from a spoon, or a specially designed, non-spill tube, with the baby sitting on your lap or in the high chair. If he really hates the medicine, or feels too ill to take anything, try using a clean dropper to squirt the medicine into the back of the mouth so that he has to swallow it.

week 28

month   date

MON
10/15 cut 2nd tooth on bottom right

TUES

WED

THURS
10/18 started to crawl

FRI

SAT

SUN

*n*OTES

GRASPING AND HOLDING

By six months your baby will be able to reach out and grasp any object within her reach provided it is not too big or too small. She will seem to assess the size of each object before she touches it and may even appear to know how heavy it is. Some babies at around six months seem unable to touch any object without grasping it: your nose or hair may come in for some rough treatment!

If you offer her another object, she will drop the one she is already holding. You may have to trick her into letting go of an object you do not want her to have by offering something else.

At this stage the more interesting things she has to touch and hold the better. Brightly colored rattles which make a noise are an obvious choice. She will enjoy feeling for different shapes and for new textures other than plastic. You can buy toys using textured materials or make your own 'feely board' by sticking on materials with different textural qualities such as corduroy, velvet, something fluffy and something slippery like silk.

*Y*ou and your baby will probably have worked out some kind of routine by now, based around her sleep and mealtimes. However, you may want to vary things a little or there may be times of the day when your baby seems bored or fretful and you don't really know what to do. The mothers of wakeful babies find it particularly hard to fill up the day with activities that amuse the baby while getting work done themselves.

It is a good idea to make one outing a day. If you need to go shopping, choose a time of day when the baby has just slept so that you don't waste sleeping time by her dozing off in the stroller and missing the adventure.

Your baby will take an interest in all manner of new objects at this age. You can hand her something simple like a yogurt container and, provided she hasn't seen it before, she will inspect it carefully from all angles, turn it over in her hands, drop it and pick it up again. At this age she will find almost anything you have in the house (provided it is safe to give her) more interesting than the simple toys made for her age group. Try her with things like brushes, large beads on a string, colored shiny paper, anything that can be squeezed or squeaked.

A baby of this age finds shopping trips entertaining on many different levels. There will be a lot for her to look at when you go out and you can help make shopping more enjoyable for her by giving her interesting things to do, like discarded packaging to play with or something to chew on.

TIPS FOR GETTING THROUGH THE DAY

- Don't stick too rigidly to a routine. If the baby is irritable or hungry ahead of time, give her lunch or a snack, and perhaps take a little longer over the meal than usual by introducing some new finger foods for her to investigate. If she seems tired, let her sleep early; you can plan an outing later on.
- If your baby seems bored, try doing something unexpected with her. Take her outdoors while you do some gardening or put her in the backpack while you do some housework.
- There are some excellent daytime television programs for small children. If your baby is used to the television as background noise she may just ignore it, but if she isn't, a children's program with songs and bright colors may hold her attention for a while.
- Babies love to watch other children, so visit the local playground or park where she can watch them. Or you can invite over a neighbor's child who can amuse the baby while you and her mother also get a break.

week 29

month   date

MON

TUES

WED

THURS

10/25 is crawling
very well & across the
room

FRI

SAT

SUN

*n*OTES

CHECKING REFERENCES

Always ask for at least two references and check them out. A written letter of reference, no matter how glowing, is not sufficient. A previous employer may be motivated to write an excellent letter of reference for a caregiver for any number of reasons. When you contact them:

● Verify the caregiver's dates of employment, childcare and household responsibilities during that time, and reasons for leaving. Clear up any discrepancies.

● Ascertain that the person applying for your job is not a friend or relative of the reference.

● Ask if the caregiver was honest, responsible, and good in emergencies?

● Did they see eye-to-eye on how children should be raised, disciplined, toilet trained, comforted, etc.?

● How well did the caregiver communicate with the employer and handle problems when they arose?

Don't forget Forming a babysitting pool or cooperative can be an excellent way of getting reliable childcare for free.

*i*N-HOME CHILDCARE

*f*inding a dependable baby-sitter or full-time childcare person, despite rumors to the contrary, involves work and more than a little luck. It can seem a daunting experience at first – negotiating your way through the baby-sitter and childcare channels, but ultimately, when you succeed in finding the right person, your life – and your child's – will probably be enriched.

Baby-sitters are usually young teenagers, college students, or mature persons who help out on an as-needed, part-time basis. They are paid by the hour. The best way to find them is by word of mouth; ask neighbors who have young children or teenagers. If that fails, try: local hospitals with nursing schools; nearby colleges or universities (the job placement office or the school of education); local high schools (guidance offices often list jobs for students); the local Y (they may keep names on file); or try placing a want ad on the bulletin board at the local library or supermarket. Interview potential baby-sitters before hiring them and ask for at least two references you can call. Ask their references how many times they have used this sitter; whether the sitter has been reliable; what the sitter's responsibilities have been; whether the children enjoy him or her.

If you have a job outside the home and can afford it, a full-time, in-home caregiver may be your best option. The advantages include not having to worry about getting your child to and from day care or having to make other arrangements when your child is sick, and greater flexibility in general. But you are dependent on one person and finding competent people can be difficult. A popular in-home childcare solution is hiring an au pair (see Useful Addresses, p. 110).

PREPARING THE SITTER

- Have a new sitter come at least 30 minutes early so that you can spend some time showing him or her where things are in your home and how they work (telephone(s); fuse box; first aid kit; extra keys in case they get locked out; burglar alarm; thermostat; baby's bottles, clothes and diapers).
- Explain the baby's preferences and routines (how the baby likes to be fed, where to diaper the baby, bedtime rituals).
- Post emergency phone numbers by the phone (pediatrician, police and fire, ambulance, nearest hospital).
- Write out clearly where you can be reached and leave a phone number. Also leave the number of a neighbor.

CHOOSING A CAREGIVER

Obviously the first qualification should be that the caregiver loves and enjoys being with children, and that she shows patience, affection and understanding toward them. Parents make a common mistake in thinking that a lot of experience and education are key things to look for, particularly if their child is under one year. But there are other qualities that are important, such as energy, carefulness, cleanliness, and a willingness to provide a variety of experiences for your child that are more important. You want a person who is cooperative, and with whom you feel you can communicate.

week 30

MON

TUES

WED

THURS

FRI

SAT

SUN

_n_OTES

BABY'S PERCEPTION

If your baby drops something, she will start looking down to see where it has fallen. Instead of a dropped object 'disappearing', she will now realize that it is still there, but in a different place. At this stage, she may infuriate you by repeatedly dropping things. It is important to understand that this is part of her development, and if you hand things back as part of a game, you will delight her.

You can make the game even more interesting when your baby is in the high chair by _putting something on the floor which will make a loud noise when objects are dropped._

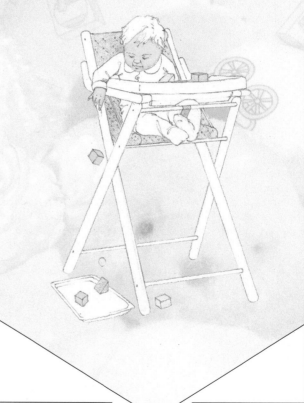

Don't forget Toys such as blocks and balls should have a diameter of at least one and one-half inches (4 cm) so that baby can't swallow them.

*a*lthough only a minority of children will be crawling well at this age, many babies will be able to move around in one way or another. You should not rely on being able to put her down and go out of the room, safe in the knowledge that she will still be in the same place when you come back. Now is the time to think about making the home safer for a mobile baby. Some of the precautions may seem premature, but remember that you will not know what your baby is capable of doing until she does it.

Make sure all dangerous objects are out of reach and similarly any small breakable objects. Fires should be screened with a fireguard,

screwed into the wall. Any unstable bookshelves or tables should be fastened in some way so that the baby cannot overturn them by bumping into them or trying to pull herself up. If you have doors with glass panels, think about putting in safety glass. Children have been seriously injured by breaking glass doors. (Safety film is illegal as a permanent glass door replacement.) Keep ashtrays or poisonous materials (bleach, paint stripper etc.) out of reach. If you have kitchen or bathroom cupboards at floor level, fit safety latches.

You will also need to use a safety harness in the baby's stroller or high chair to stop her trying to wiggle out.

STEPS AND STAIRS

If you have steps in the house – even one or two – you should put up a stair gate; make sure it is properly installed, and don't be tempted to keep climbing over it,

especially when you are carrying the baby, as this can be dangerous. If the steps are in a place where you are coming and going all the time, it may be safer

to do without a gate and make the area safe in other ways. Once your crawling baby learns to climb stairs, though, a stair gate is probably essential.

week 31

month   *date*

MON

TUES

WED

THURS

FRI

SAT

SUN

WHAT TO TAKE ON VACATION

Pack a travel bag for baby with diapers, baby wipes, a change of clothes, the baby's food and drink, one or two favorite toys and, if appropriate, something to nibble or chew on.

If you are going abroad on your vacation, check on the local availability of certain goods such as baby milks and disposable diapers, so you don't have to take two weeks' supply with you.

Take a first-aid kit containing infant acetaminophen syrup, sun protection cream with a high sun block factor, ointment for insect bites or cuts, cream for diaper rash. You may be able to get medicine to counter diarrhea with a doctor's prescription.

You may also need sterilizing tablets and possibly a gadget for boiling water in your hotel room or apartment. (You will also need to bring an electrical adaptor to work appliances on a foreign electricity circuit.)

*n*OTES

tRAVELING WITH BABY

*i*t can be difficult traveling with a baby, especially once he has become mobile and wants to explore everything. However, if you plan your trip with care it should not be too stressful, whether you are traveling by car, train or plane. Always pack a separate travel bag containing everything you need for the baby (see opposite). A backpack is an excellent way of transporting the baby on foot, or when stopping for a break.

Air travel is probably the most difficult with a young child, as there is little room to change diapers and nowhere for him to crawl or sit (except your lap). You can reserve a sky-crib on long distance flights – ask when you make your booking. You will then usually be seated in part of the aircraft where there is room for the sky-crib to be attached. Give the baby a drink or breast-feed him at takeoff and landing to prevent the pressure building up in his ears and causing pain; this is particularly important if he has a cold.

If you are traveling by car, try to time your journey to fit in with your baby's nap and mealtimes to make the trip easier for everyone. You can buy a plastic tray which fits on to some car safety seats, enabling you to give the baby something to eat and toys to play with. Break your journey frequently to give a mobile baby a chance to let off steam. Always stop for a while if he is irritable; few people can really concentrate on driving with a screaming baby in the back of the car.

See Week 18
for Games to Play

See Week 30
for Family
Vacations

See Week 46
for Safety and
First-Aid

KEEPING BABY AMUSED

In the car
- Play 'Peekaboo' over the front car seat if you are not driving.
- Keep a supply of interesting objects in the front to hand to the baby one at a time when he gets bored.
- Hang a toy which the baby can operate from the coat hook or roof of the car.
- Sing songs, clap hands or play a musical tape.

On a train
- Walk in the corridor and look out of the windows.
- Play 'Pat-a-cake' and other games on your knee.
- Some trains have small fold-down tables you can use as a play-tray or a lunch table, if the people in the seats opposite don't mind.
- If your baby is getting irritable, or he finds the noise frightening, hold him firmly and soothe him – the noise and movement of the train may eventually lull him to sleep.

On a plane
- Walk the baby up and down when they are not serving drinks or meals.
- Play bouncing games on your knee.
- If you have seats with leg room at the front, put down a mat and some toys and let the baby play there.
- Keep one or two new and interesting toys on a long trip for when he's bored with everything else and you are feeling weary.

week 32

MON

TUES

WED

THURS

FRI

SAT

SUN

*n*OTES

VACATION EQUIPMENT

- Pack a travel bag with your baby's things and keep it handy on the trip.
- Take a light, folding stroller if you are traveling with a loaded car or by train or plane.
- You may need a comfortable sling or back (frame) pack if you are going walking.
- You can get portable child seats in several forms – some clip or screw onto the side of a table, booster seats fit on top of a chair, and cloth traveling seats fit over the back of a chair.
- A portable crib will be essential if a crib is not provided. Where a crib is provided, check that it has the safety features described in Week 11, Choosing a Crib.

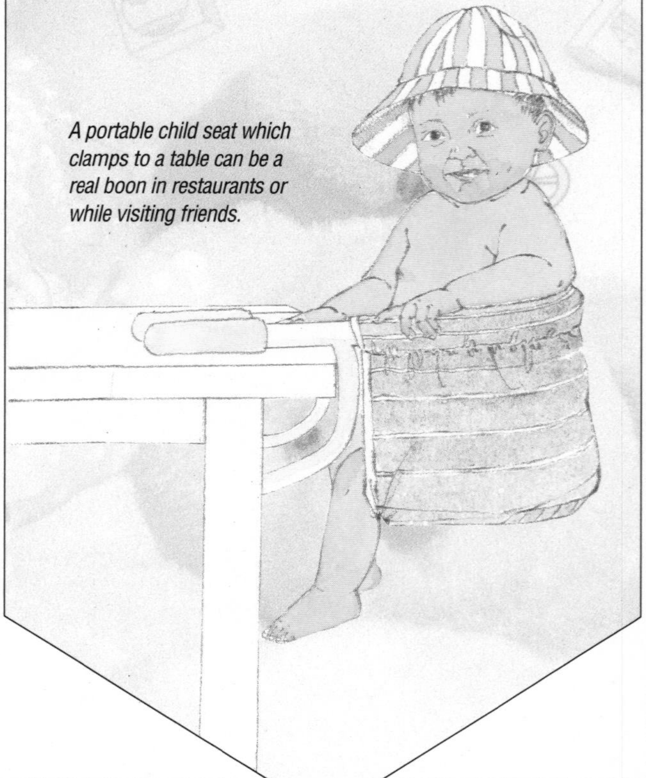

A portable child seat which clamps to a table can be a real boon in restaurants or while visiting friends.

Don't forget Take sun screen lotions, sun hats and sun umbrella for vacations in the sun.

*f*AMILY VACATIONS

*a*t some point in your baby's first year you are likely to go away on vacation as a family. It is worth giving some thought as to what kind of vacation will be best, and to accept that you might settle for a very different kind of vacation from the type you had as a couple.

If you want to go out in the evenings, you will have to go somewhere where babysitting is available. If you go to a hotel, you will need to check whether they have facilities for babies and perhaps a babysitting service, so that you can eat your evening meal without worrying whether the baby will wake and cry. You may also want to know if they cater to children in other ways – high chairs in the dining room and a crib and bedding so you don't have to take your own.

Young children often react badly to heat, so beware of going anywhere very hot. Babies easily develop rashes like prickly heat and their delicate skin burns readily in hot sun. A beach vacation may be ruined by your baby's inability to sleep on hot nights – especially if you are all in a small room together and have neighbors partying at 2 a.m.! If your baby is bottle-fed, take the formula that she is used to.

Seaside vacations may seem ideal, but in the first year your baby is unlikely to appreciate it all that much. Many babies will sit on the beach in the shade and play happily with a bucket and spade, at least for a while. But others eat the sand and pebbles on the beach. It is unlikely that you will be able to spend the whole day on the beach without her getting terribly bored.

Any vacation that involves you in much traveling, apart from getting there and back, is likely to be difficult. But walking vacations can be successful if you have a comfortable backpack in which to carry the baby – most interesting walks will take you over paths where a stroller will be worse than useless.

See Week 31 for Traveling with Baby

VACATION CHOICE

Hotel
✔ If you pick the right hotel, you will have a real rest. There will be built-in babysitting and meals will be prepared for you.

✗ Possible problems with neighboring guests if your baby cries at night. Usually restricted room space.

Rental units with kitchens
✔ Generally cheaper; easier to follow your home routine. Neighbors should be less of a problem.

✗ It may be difficult to find a baby-sitter if you want to go out. More work for you, especially if there is no washing machine.

Camping/Camper
✔ Some campsites or trailer sites are geared up with facilities for children. The baby will enjoy plenty of fresh air.

✗ More work for you – possible problems with neighbors if baby is noisy at night and if there is no safe, enclosed space.

week 33

MON
_____

TUES
_____

WED
_____

THURS
_____

FRI
_____

SAT
_____

SUN
_____

*n*OTES

BATHING THE OLDER BABY

Once your baby has been sitting without support for some time, he will probably want to sit up in the bath and play with his toys. Brightly colored boats and ducks are fun, but best of all are containers which can pour, fill and empty. Stacking cups, some with holes in the bottom, are ideal, or you can use empty plastic bottles.

To make bathtime safer, put a rubber non-slip mat in the bath or buy a support to help a newly sitting baby stay upright. Never leave a baby unattended in the bath in case he slips or falls.

It may still be safer and more economical to use the baby bath at this stage. You can put it inside the big bath to get your baby used to that environment and it won't matter if there is a lot of splashing.

*d*EVELOPING SKILLS

Children are individuals and as such develop at their own pace and in their own way. Your pediatrician or family practitioner will, in all likelihood, perform periodic screenings of your child's development. These are normally done in conjunction with well-baby visits and routine checkups.

If your child's development is lagging in any area, your doctor will closely monitor it and he or you may want to have a more comprehensive assessment done at a university hospital or clinic. In some states, developmental screenings are available free of charge for pre-school age children through the school district.

See Week 7 for Well-baby examinations

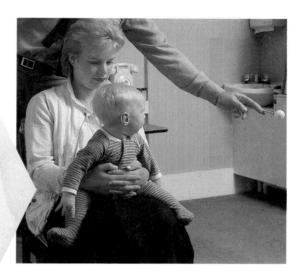

You may start to notice that your baby jumps or looks around whenever there is a sudden noise. She may also look up at you if you make a sound she associates either with food – perhaps a spoon scraping a dish or the kettle boiling – or with some other pleasurable event, such as Daddy opening the front door. If she is showing these kinds of responses at home but doesn't respond to the doctor's testing, ask for another test to be carried out.

BABY'S HEARING/VISION

Hearing and vision problems can interfere with your child's development. For example, normal speech development depends on the ability to hear well. For this reason, at your well-baby visits and during routine visits in the preschool years your doctor will be doing periodic hearing and vision tests on your child.

The American Medical Association recommends that ideally, children should have hearing and vision screenings at eight months and nine months, at three years and at five years. But if you note anything that concerns you about your baby's hearing or vision, don't hesitate to speak with your doctor. If, for example, at eight months your baby does not turn toward a whispered voice or the sound of a rattle, or if she constantly favors one eye when looking at an object, you should mention this to your doctor. It is best that any problems with hearing or vision are picked up as early as possible so that any necessary corrective treatment can begin immediately.

week 34

month _____ *date* _____

MON
_____

_____

TUES
_____

_____

WED
_____

_____

THURS
_____

_____

FRI
_____

_____

SAT
_____

_____

SUN
_____

_____

*n*OTES

FINGER FOODS

Many babies enjoy finger foods that they can pick up and eat themselves. Try giving different foods in this form, such as the ideas below. Babies of this age may like small items such as peas which they can eat one at a time when they have mastered the pincer grip (see Week 38). Use cookie cutters to make more interesting shapes from cheese, bread or cooked potato.

fEEDING THE OLDER BABY

by this stage your baby will probably be getting much of her nourishment from solid food and milk will have become an additional drink rather than a basic, although it remains an excellent source of protein and vitamins. If your baby is slow in switching over to solids and still prefers milk, don't worry; at this age she can do perfectly well on breast- and formula milk provided she gets some solid food as well, particularly foods containing iron such as egg yolk, dried fruits and red meat. If you want to wean your baby off milk, though, try offering it in a cup rather than a bottle and only give it after, not between, meals if she still seems interested.

Provided the baby's diet is balanced overall, you need not feel that every meal has to be perfectly balanced in itself. It is quite all right to have protein at one meal, and bread, or potato and vegetables, at another. Your baby will probably be ready for lumpier foods, stronger flavors and thicker textures.

Feeding herself allows the baby to eat as much as she wants as quickly as she wants, which will help to avoid mealtime problems later. Put newspaper down on the floor under the high chair, put a bib on your baby and let her get on with it. If you have two spoons, one for the baby and one for you, you can scoop up food which misses her mouth and pop it in, and you can feed her if she gets too frustrated. Some babies like to get hold of the food in their fingers and simply play with it. It is important that you let them do this, at least from time to time, preferably at the end of a meal. It won't take long to wipe down the baby and the high chair when he has finished.

Whenever possible, sit down and eat with your baby. She may enjoy tasting a mouthful or two of your meal and may offer you some of hers. Eating together will help her think that mealtimes are fun. When she indicates that she has had enough and turns her head away, don't force food on her or she may start resisting all solid food.

See Week 42 for Weaning to a Cup

Many babies want to feed themselves at this stage. This is very messy, but do encourage it, because it will help her coordination and this freedom will make mealtimes happier for her.

week 35

month   *date*

MON

TUES

WED

THURS

FRI

SAT

SUN

*n*OTES

LEARNING TO CRAWL

Babies are varied in the age at which they learn to crawl. Some never learn to crawl at all but go straight from sitting and perhaps bottom-shuffling to walking.

Learning to crawl can be a frustrating process for some babies. They may be able to get up on hands and knees but then rock, unable to make any progress, and fall down on their faces. Others may try to pull themselves along with their arms but then end up shuffling backwards.

Some babies learn to crawl on their stomachs. A few crawl on hands and feet like a bear. Other babies who cannot actually crawl get around well by a combination of rolling over, shuffling and 'creeping' backwards.

Your baby may take all his weight on his arms and legs but still be unable to move forward. Eventually he will master the technique – much to his delight.

*t*OYS FOR THE OLDER BABY

*a*t around eight months your baby will be developing fast. He needs to handle as many different objects as possible to find out what they do. Until recently, his main use for toys or any objects within reach was to put them in his mouth. Now he is beginning to experiment and explore what can be done with them. He will bang things, shake them, pick them up and drop them, pull them and stroke them.

He is also beginning to understand how a thing works once it has been demonstrated. If you press a button and a toy squeaks, he will try to press it too. If you are writing with a pen, he may grab the pen and try to 'write' as well as trying to put it in his mouth. He may become interested in toys with movable parts or those which come apart. He will enjoy handling things with lots of knobs and those with different textures and others which make a distinctive noise.

A baby of this age can be happy on the floor or in his playpen for quite long periods provided he has enough to amuse him. Besides toys, you can give him things like cardboard boxes, containers of all kinds, old magazines to crumble, tear and chew, saucepans and wooden spoons,

and scraps of material. Toys designed for older children, provided they are safe, have great appeal for many babies (cars with wheels that go round and doors that open, for example). If he is playing with anything that could be dangerous if broken, like a string of beads, keep a watchful eye on him.

Once your baby enjoys looking at brightly colored pictures and likes opening and shutting things, this may be the time to buy a few simple board books of different sizes or shapes. A small thick book, a large flat one and another which folds out will keep a baby of this age busy. Board books are also good for a teething baby to chew on. You can get plastic books which go in the bath, and rag books which can be washed when they get grubby. You can begin to point out colors, shapes and objects when you read to your baby.

week 36

MON

TUES

WED

THURS

FRI

SAT

SUN

*n*OTES

SAFETY AT HOME

Your baby will be developing new skills such as pulling herself up to a standing position and climbing up on the stairs and furniture. You should have anticipated this stage by putting dangerous objects out of reach and fixing any furniture which might topple over. Use a safety gate on the stairs. Cover electrical sockets with childproof safety covers and fix safety latches to cupboard doors and drawers. Buy a safety latch for the refrigerator, too.

Now that your baby is more mobile it is even more important to make sure that she is strapped into her high chair or stroller. It is worth strapping very active babies into a supermarket cart too. Never be tempted not to strap a baby into her car safety seat, no matter how violent and stressful the protest.

*t*IME FOR YOURSELF

s your baby gets older you may begin to feel that you have far too little time for yourself or for your partner. After the baby is in bed and the meal has been cooked and eaten, the toys put away and chores done, you may want to do nothing else but go to bed. If you have already gone back to work, there will be even less time to devote to yourself.

It is important that you feel happy and fulfilled – otherwise you cannot enjoy your baby or your relationship with your partner. It is worth setting aside a special time each week which you spend with your partner, uncluttered by domestic chores. Perhaps you could also arrange to have one evening a week off by yourself, to visit friends or perhaps to go to an evening class. Your partner might like an evening to go out with friends or play some sport. If you have agreed on this in advance and you both have your own time, you will not resent the fact that one of you seems to go out more than the other.

It is worth establishing some kind of regular evening babysitting arrangement, either with a relative, with a neighbor whom you know and trust or perhaps with friends who have babies of a similar age so that you can babysit for one another. Some areas have a babysitting cooperative whereby a group of people who know one another can babysit in exchange for points or tokens per hour. Going out together without the baby can help revive the feelings you shared before you had the baby.

Your health and looks are also important, so devote some time to them. Make sure that you eat well and that you are getting all the minerals and vitamins you need.

See Week 14 for Leaving Baby at Home

See Week 30 for Safety and the Mobile Baby

TEN-MINUTE IDEAS

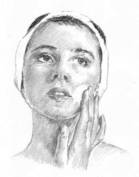

- Run a deep bath, put some foaming bath gel in it and enjoy a relaxing soak.
- Manicure and paint your fingernails – and/or your toenails.
- Give yourself a face massage to leave your skin tingling. Massage your face, chin and neck, using cold cream or massage cream.

- Apply a fast-acting facial for deep and thorough cleansing.
- Lie on the bed, or sit in a comfortable chair, to read a magazine, a chapter of your book, or the newspaper, in complete peace.
- Practice some deep breathing, or some relaxing yoga exercises.

week 37

month	date

MON

TUES

WED

THURS

FRI

SAT

SUN

PLAYING PEEKABOO!

This becomes many babies' favorite game at this age and is one which can be infinitely adapted.

Cover your face with your hands and then take them away or peer round them. Or look up from a book, magazine or newspaper held between you and the baby (you might manage to read a few lines in between!) The baby himself may discover he can hide behind something and become the active party in this new, exciting game.

notes

*e*QUIPPING THE OLDER BABY

*y*our baby's needs start to change as he becomes more active. His clothes will be subjected to much more wear and tear as he crawls about on the floor and 'furniture' that was once safe and secure should be replaced with sturdier equipment that can be used for the next eighteen months or so. The Moses basket, for example, is no longer stable enough. He may roll out of it. A bouncing chair is dangerous once he can sit forward and reach out.

CLOTHES

It is good for a crawling baby, and one who is learning to stand and feel his feet to go barefoot indoors when he can; socks may be necessary in cold weather, however, and you can get lined fabric booties with non-slip soles. At this stage he may prefer trousers or overalls to all-in-one suits; when a baby crawls his feet can work out of the toes of a suit and get caught up. Overalls are usually good value; they can be adjusted at the shoulders and some have snaps up the inside legs which makes diaper changing easier.

Jogging suits with separate tops and bottoms are also comfortable for a baby who is mobile. If you do buy a stretch suit, look for those which allow you to change diapers without having to take the whole garment off. Some have a flap in the back, others a zipper or snaps which go right down the leg.

EQUIPMENT

This is the time to buy either a low-chair or high chair to feed your baby in; a high chair or one which converts is probably the best buy. Some models fold into a small chair and table for the toddler; others simply lift off a high stand to be used on the floor as a play chair.

You might consider a portable crib for taking away with you or for when you want your baby to

stay with friends or relatives for an afternoon or overnight. Portable cribs come in many different shapes; make sure the sides are high enough and that the base is firm, or it will be unsuitable for an active toddler.

A lightweight folding stroller will come into its own now; it is easy to take on public transportation, in the trunk of a car or on a plane. You may find it worth investing in an inexpensive, simple model if your carriage or stroller combination is very heavy or takes up a lot of space even when folded.

week 38

month   *date*

MON

TUES

WED

THURS

FRI

SAT

SUN

*n*OTES

MANUAL DEXTERITY

Up to now your baby has only been able to take hold of objects by scooping with her whole hand and picking them up in her palm. From now on, however, she will learn to poke at things with one finger and to pick up small objects between forefinger and thumb, in 'the pincer grip'. Once your baby has acquired this skill, she will love anything that she can pick up in this way. Give her small bits of food to eat like peas, crumbs of bread or grains of cereal.

The mobile baby may crawl around the room picking up all the tiny bits of fluff or dirt she can find on the floor or carpet. These too will go straight into her mouth, so it is important to keep the floor clean. Make sure that there are no small objects left on the floor which could cause her to choke, such as pins, buttons or tiny pieces of Lego.

*t*HE CLINGING BABY

*a*t around this age many babies develop what is known as separation anxiety. They become very clingy and cry every time you put them down, step out of the room, or go out of sight. A mobile baby may crawl around after you wherever you go and a baby who cannot crawl may cry piteously when you move away. Even a baby who has been quite happy to stay with a known person, or to play on her own for a while, may suddenly hate being left even for short periods. A baby who becomes very anxious may continue to want her mother constantly with her until some time well into the second year. While it is distressing to leave a baby who is crying for your return, be reassured that tears will quickly stop once you are out of sight.

Sometimes babies continue to show anxiety every time you leave them because they sense that you yourself are nervous about leaving them. This is only reinforced if you change your mind and decide not to leave her after all because she is crying. It is important to realize that almost all babies cry on separation from their mothers but that this is usually short-lived, and won't do her any harm. Babies protest much less if they are left with someone they know and in a familiar and comfortable environment.

If you are at home with your baby, you may find it hard that she still clings to you and cries whenever you step inside the bathroom or outside the back door. Almost the only thing you can do about this phase is to accept it and to take her with you as much as possible, or at least keep her in your sight.

See Week 14 for Leaving Baby at Home

See Week 29 for Going Back to Work

A baby left in the care of a familiar figure with plenty to amuse her, and whose daily routine is followed, is unlikely to be unhappy for long.

MAKING IT EASIER

If your baby is clingy, get her used to spending short periods with another known person, perhaps her father, a grandparent, or a friend she sees often. You could have the friend's baby one morning a week in return. Once she begins to accept that you sometimes leave and that you do return, this will stand you in good stead if you ever have to leave her unexpectedly.

When you leave her, do so quickly and cheerfully to show there is nothing to worry about and that crying won't make you change your mind.

If your baby likes to be carried and you have to put her down to get on with household tasks, try to turn them into a game for her. Play 'peekaboo' while you are washing, or tickle her in the middle of the dusting. Talk to her as you work, to show that you're not ignoring her.

week 39

MON

TUES

WED

THURS

FRI

SAT

SUN

NOTES

HAND COORDINATION

By this age your baby will be able to use both his hands together. Instead of discarding one object when handed a second, he may hold them both and compare them. He may play with them together, banging them, putting them down together and then picking them up again. He is learning to let go of things in a controlled way by unclenching his fingers.

He will also be able to pass an object from one hand to another. His movements have become less haphazard and are more coordinated as he acquires greater control of his fingers. He will soon be able to wave from the wrist.

Your baby will be interested in seeing whether one object will fit inside another and will spend a lot of time working out what fits where.

He may learn to point at things he wants and to hold up his arms if he wants you to pick him up.

Don't forget You should have installed safety latches and a stair gate by now.

KEEPING BABY AMUSED

*a*s your baby gets older, sleeps less and becomes more mobile, you may find yourself trying to think of ways to amuse him. Babies soon become bored with the limited selection of toys available at home. If you are at home with your baby, you obviously can't expect him to amuse himself with toys all the time while you do housework. Try to create times every day when you play with your baby – if you meet his demands for attention then, he will be more likely to play by himself at other times.

An outing to the local playground can be exciting for your baby. He may be a little fearful the first time he goes on a slide or a swing. Hold him firmly and he will soon realize that it can be great fun.

ACTIVITIES TO ENJOY TOGETHER

There are lots of outside activities the enterprising mother can enjoy with her baby. This can be an ideal age to start taking them swimming. Some swimming pools have specially heated pools for younger children and regular sessions for mothers and babies. Babies who are prone to ear infections or congestion, or who suffer from eczema, are better kept out of the pool for a little longer.

Babies also enjoy visiting playgrounds designed for older children. Once a baby can sit up firmly he will enjoy a toddler swing which encloses him safely, especially if you say 'boo' or tickle him when he swings close to you. Going with mother on a slide can also be great fun.

Your local YWCA may organize special sessions for young children with trampolines, indoor slides and other equipment which a surprisingly young baby can enjoy. All these places are also good for meeting other mothers and children.

See Week 35 for Toys for the Older Baby

ACTION RHYMES

Pat-a-cake, pat-a-cake, baker's man
Bake me a cake as fast as you can
Prick it and pat it and mark it with 'B'
And put it in the oven for baby and me.
Clap baby's hands in rhythm and imitate kneading.

Clap hands, daddy comes
With his pockets full of plums.
Clap hand in rhythm and mime taking something out of a pocket – draw a large circle in the air for 'plums'.
Mime taking the imaginary plum out from behind your ear or from your mouth and pop it in his.

To market, to market; to buy a fat pig,
Home again, home again, jiggety jig
To market, to market, to buy a fat hog
Home again, home again, jiggety jog.
Put baby on your knee and jiggle him to the rhythm.

week 40

MON

TUES

WED

THURS

FRI

SAT

SUN

COPYCAT

At this age your baby will probably start imitating gestures that you make, such as clapping hands and waving. Help her to copy such gestures by playing games like 'Peekaboo'.

The baby will also copy some of your gestures unconsciously, such as shaking her head to say 'no' or drawing back and frowning when she sees something she doesn't like. Don't forget that wooden spoons, paper towel spools, cardboard boxes and tins to bang all make good toys. Your baby will love to have her own handbag and keys, too! If your baby is mobile, she will enjoy playing a simple game of 'hide and seek' with you.

Your baby may find it funny to clap her hands to copy you.

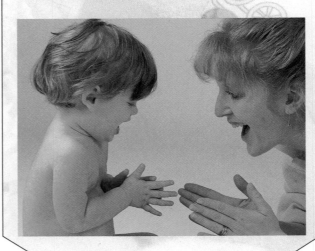

NOTES

SLEEP PROBLEMS

Whether your baby has never slept through the night, or has slept well from an early age, sleep problems can develop. These may occur even in a formerly good sleeper because of her anxiety at being separated from you. A habit of waking in the night may develop after an illness, during which your baby woke frequently and was nursed by you or taken into your bed. Even a baby who is very tired at bedtime can now resist sleep. She may protest loudly at being put down and continue to cry for long periods.

It is necessary to sort out a consistent way of dealing with this phase, to reassure your baby that there is nothing to be afraid of and that you have not deserted her – but that it is bedtime. It may help to define the bedtime routine you follow at this time.

Take time over her supper, play a quick game or two with her before her bath. You could sing a lullaby as you get her ready for bed to put her in a calm frame of mind. Put on her diaper and night clothes in the same place, then carry her to her crib. If you have a mobile, perhaps look at that together, then give her a cuddle and the bottle- or breast-feeding – and put her to bed. If she cries, give her a few minutes to settle, then go back and rub her back or stroke her hair – but don't pick her up again. Keep going back at regular intervals till she goes to sleep.

If your baby wakes frequently in the night, try the same technique. Go in briefly to let her know that you are there, and check that there is nothing wrong, then leave her. If she continues to cry, go back to check every so often, perhaps leaving it a little longer each time. Remember that you need your sleep and it won't hurt her to cry a little, as long as she knows you are there.

See Week 26 for Eating and Sleeping

If your baby feels safe and contented in her crib, she may spend long periods playing happily, allowing you to get more rest.

EARLY WAKERS

If your baby wakes early in the morning, you may be able to keep her amused by putting toys and interesting objects in or near the crib. A musical toy or an activity center which she can operate herself are very good for this purpose. Some babies, however, seem to want attention from the moment they wake. Taking her into your bed may please her and give you a rest.

You could try shifting her bedtime to a slightly later time, only half an hour or so, to give you a little longer in the mornings. This usually works if you are persistent – bear in mind that for the first few days she is likely to wake at the usual time anyway.

week 41

MON

TUES

WED

THURS

FRI

SAT

SUN

ENCOURAGING SPEECH

The most important way in which you can help your baby to speak is to talk to him, sing to him and play verbal games with him. He needs this one-to-one contact to develop his speech and, above all, to teach him that talking is fun. Remember to name objects in everyday use and repeat them so that he learns their meaning. Ask him questions such as 'Do you want a drink?' just before you pour one.

At around nine months your baby will start to 'take part' in adult discussions. Often he will try to join in, laughing when you laugh, making loud exclamations or babbling away himself.

Babies vary greatly in the age at which they start to use real words, so don't be too anxious if you can't make out any words by the end of the first year. They understand a great deal of your speech before learning to talk themselves, so it's more important to check that he understands you and responds to your voice.

*n*OTES

COMMUNICATION

Although most babies don't produce their first intelligible word until at least their first birthday, preparation for speech starts earlier. From six weeks he will have been making cooing sounds and by around six months the familiar 'babble' begins. At all these stages you can encourage your child to develop speech by talking back and responding. Let him enjoy the sounds he makes and help him to feel that he is communicating something.

A baby also needs to use his mouth in different ways to learn how to make sounds and develop the muscles that are needed to form noises. Too much sucking on pacifiers and bottles can deter the baby from developing these muscles; breast-feeding on the other hand will have given him a good start as it develops strong muscles in the mouth and jaw. Babies should also get used to biting and chewing food and getting their tongues around different textures.

Somewhere around nine or ten months babies learn to get what they want by pointing. This is a big step in learning to communicate and also in developing language, since when the baby points, the mother can give the object a name. He may come to understand several words even if he is unable to speak them and will find a way of clearly showing that he understands; if you say 'clap' he may clap his hands and when you say, 'bye bye', wave his hand.

See Week 50 for First Words

Looking at books together is a good way to introduce your baby to new words, other than those he hears every day. Name each picture for him, as you turn the pages, and he will soon try to repeat the sounds back to you.

BABY LANGUAGE

At about nine months a baby's babble becomes more complicated as different sounds creep in. He may invent little words which mean little to anybody else but you and him.

Your baby may sometimes sound as if he is actually talking, but in a foreign language! Interestingly, the babble of children from different countries appears to be broadly similar, and is little influenced by the language the baby hears. Similarly, deaf children often babble quite normally and speech problems occur only later.

You may find it difficult to distinguish your baby's first words because they are not clear and are only approximations of the real word. However, a baby is using a 'word' if he uses the same sound to indicate the same object. He may, for example, say 'da' when he wants a drink from his cup, or 'tu' for shoe. Because it is easer to say, 'dada' often comes before 'mama' much to many mothers' disgust!

week 42

month _____ *date* _____

MON

_____

TUES

_____

WED

_____

THURS

_____

FRI

_____

SAT

_____

SUN

_____

*n*OTES

STANDING

At around ten months your baby may start pulling herself into the upright position using furniture or people as support. Her balance will, however, be very poor and she will easily fall over – she needs to cling on with both hands.

Once your baby can pull herself up, she may have a problem because she is unable to sit down again. She will eventually learn to let go and sit down with a bump: you can help by giving her something soft to land on. She will lose confidence if she hurts herself.

If you support your baby under her arms, she will probably start to take steps and 'walk' across the floor. Hold her very firmly because her balance is still precarious. Don't get trapped into spending hours walking up and down with your baby. It can be very tiring for you and won't help your baby walk unaided.

*W*EANING TO A CUP

When your baby is about nine months old you will probably want to start weaning her from breast or bottle for all but early morning or night feedings. If you have introduced a cup earlier, there should be no problem in offering a drink from a cup instead of a bottle at mealtimes or in between.

Many babies drink more than they actually need because sucking from a bottle gives them comfort. A baby who feeds from the breast for comfort often still gets a lot of her nourishment from breast-milk and may be reluctant to take other drinks or much solid food. So when you first offer the cup regularly you may find that your baby appears to drink less than usual, but this is not a cause for concern: she will not let herself go thirsty for long.

Babies vary greatly in their need to suck for comfort, and some mothers will find that they can drop all breast- or bottle-feedings around the end of the first year. Some babies love their bedtime feeding, however, and are not ready to give it up at this stage; if you don't want your baby to have a bottle after the age of one, then get her used to a cup early and cut down bottles gradually. Drinking from a cup is much less likely to damage your baby's teeth than drinking from a bottle, so this is a habit that is worth encouraging early.

Today there are excellent plastic cups with spouts which the baby has to half-suck, half-drink, which makes weaning to a cup easier than it used to be. Some have handles, some not, and some are weighted at the bottom to help prevent them tipping over; in some the fluid comes out more quickly than others.

You can give your baby milk, or water if she will drink it. Dilute fruit juices with three or four parts of water as undiluted fruit juice is slightly acid and may not be very thirst quenching either. Once your baby is used to undiluted juice it will be harder to get her to accept more dilute drinks.

See Week 24
for Using a Cup

See Week 50
for Weaning
from Breast or
Bottle

CHANGING SLEEP PATTERNS

Towards the end of the first year your baby's sleeping pattern may alter as she needs less sleep. A baby who had two good naps a day may wake after a shorter period or drop one nap altogether. Often the baby's morning nap will get later so that you are either giving her an early lunch or letting your baby sleep through her lunchtime and perhaps wake too early from her nap because she is hungry.

You can't make your baby sleep unless she is tired, so you may just have to accept that there will be times when her routine alters and be prepared to adjust. If you time naps right, so that your baby is really tired before you put her down, she may go to sleep without any trouble, whereas twenty minutes earlier she would have made a fuss.

Even if she is not ready to sleep, put her in her crib with toys to play with. Let her grumble or cry for a short while – she may amuse herself for some time even if she does not actually go to sleep.

week 43

month　　　　　*date*

MON

TUES

WED

THURS

FRI

SAT

SUN

Feeding himself is a big step towards baby's sense of independence and you should encourage it from an early age. If your baby feeds himself, he will take only as much as he needs and will not be tempted to overeat or, if you press food on him, reject food and become a difficult and fussy eater.

Give your baby a large, comfortable bib, put newspaper on the floor, give him a spoon – and let him go for it. Use unbreakable bowls, preferably with a suction base. When he stops trying to eat and starts smearing food everywhere or throwing it on the floor, don't scold him, simply end the meal, clean him up and take him out of the high chair.

*n*OTES

*t*HE OLDER BABY'S DIET

*y*our baby may now be eating a more or less adult diet, except that you should use no salt and reduce the sugar in cooking, and you will still need to mash or chop food appropriately. The textures your baby can cope with will depend partly on how many teeth are through; a late teether will find it much harder to manage raw apples, carrots and crusts than one whose teeth are through ahead of time. Some babies actively dislike lumpy food, but may prefer to help themselves to chopped pieces of food.

It will save you time if you adapt the food that you cook for yourselves for your baby, perhaps adding more salt or sugar after you have removed his portion. Avoid foods that are too rich, such as those with quantities of added cream and butter in them.

When buying convenience foods, check the ingredients carefully and try to avoid artificial colorings, flavorings and sweeteners, and check that they do not contain too much salt and sugar. Always buy the healthier version of a product: for example, choose brown rather than white rice, and ice cream made with cream, milk and eggs and with real fruit, rather than ice cream made from non-milk fat with artificial colorings and flavorings, which is far less nutritious for your baby.

If you buy a lot of commercial baby foods, do try to vary these as much as possible and make sure you buy foods appropriate for your baby's age. Buying food this way is likely to be quite expensive but at least you will know the meals are well-balanced, should not contain any harmful ingredients and have all the necessary vitamins added.

See Week 34 for Feeding the Older Baby

FOOD ADDITIVES – BEWARE!

Today's foods contain several thousand chemical additives in the form of artificial colorings, flavorings, preservatives, and sweeteners. Fortunately, the vast majority of these additives are safe. But some of them are not, and have not been banned.

Other additives have yet to be fully tested before we can know whether they are safe or not. Parents need to scrutinize food labels carefully. According to the Center for Science in the Public Interest (see Useful Addresses, p. 110), the food that children eat, especially, should be as free from these 'Top Ten' additives as possible:

- **Acesulfame K** – a sugar substitute found in beverages, gelatin desserts, puddings.
- **Artificial colorings** – Select, whenever possible, foods without dyes. Avoid Yellow No. 5 and Red No. 3, in particular.
- **Aspartame** – a sugar substitute sold commercially as Equal and NutraSweet.
- **BHA** – added to oil-containing foods to prevent oxidation and retard rancidity.
- **BHT** – closely related to BHA, and used for the same purposes.
- **Caffeine** – found naturally in tea, coffee, and cocoa, and added to many soft drinks.
- **Monosodium Glutamate (MSG)** – found in some Chinese food and hydrolized vegetable protein.
- **Nitrate and Nitrite** – used as preservatives in meats.
- **Saccharin** – a sugar substitute.
- **Sulfites** – used to prevent discoloration in dried fruits.

week 44

month   *date*

MON

TUES

WED

THURS

FRI

SAT

SUN

*n*OTES

LOSING AND FINDING

At around this age a baby will be interested in letting go and looking for lost objects. She realizes that just because something has disappeared from her vision doesn't mean it's no longer there. She will drop things from her high chair and then bend over the edge to see where they have gone. If you hide an object under a bowl, or cushion, she will know it is underneath and will enjoy removing whatever is concealing it to see the object reappear.

You can make up many games which play on your baby's new discovery, such as hiding different objects under stacking cups, and playing 'Which hand is it in?' She will love to try and open your hand to see what is there.

Your baby will be thrilled if you join in hide-and-seek games with her. It is amusing to see that the baby's idea of hiding is simply to conceal her head and not the rest of her body. You can play games like this with your baby at the same time as you get on with the housework.

*t*HE FRUSTRATED BABY

*a*t around this age your baby – and you as parents – may discover that she has a will of her own, when she realizes that she is not able or allowed to do many of the things that she would like to do. Once she becomes mobile she may wish to explore every room of the house and open and shut every cupboard and container, remove the contents of every drawer and take to pieces anything that comes apart. You will need to create an environment that is safe but which frustrates her as little as possible. Getting dressed is often a time of intense resistance. She may stiffen her limbs and make your job as difficult as possible. You need to remain patient.

A frustrated baby may resent being dressed or having her diaper changed or being ignored when she is bored or lonely.

LIMITING THE PROBLEMS

Fortunately a baby of this age is easily distracted and you will quickly be able to switch her attention from the forbidden object to something else. Taking the baby to another room or playing a game which commands her attention can make her forget something that she wanted to do. Some temptations will simply have to be removed or made safe, however, to prevent her heading for them every time they catch her eye.

Saying 'no'
Despite all your safety precautions, there will be times when you will have to say 'no', and at this age you can begin to teach your baby the meaning of this word. For some time she will have sensed approval or disapproval in your voice and you can use your voice to reinforce the message as you remove either her or the object which is forbidden. However, not all babies react in the same way; some treat 'no' as a challenging game and repeat what they have been told not to do; others burst into tears. You can't expect a baby of this age to respond to a spoken command – you can only use it to back up your actions. If she learns by experience that she is really not allowed to empty the contents of the fruit bowl, she will eventually give up trying.

Physical limitations
If your baby wants to crawl but hasn't quite got the hang of it, or if she has mastered standing up but hasn't worked out how to sit down again without falling over, she is clearly going to be very frustrated with the limitations of her own body.

Try to make other things as easy as possible for her so she doesn't have too many frustrations to deal with. Find ways of helping her to achieve things she wants to do; for example, allow her to feed herself or help to transport her to where she wants to go, to give her a feeling of achievement and self-confidence.

See Week 30 for Safety and the Mobile Baby

93

week 45

month　　　　*date*

MON

_____

TUES

_____

WED

_____

THURS

_____

FRI

_____

SAT

_____

SUN

_____

*n*OTES

'CRUISING'

Once your baby has learned to pull himself up to a standing position he will soon start walking, using his hands to support him. This is known as cruising. At first he will progress slowly, and will need to hold on to something.

Next, he will take more weight on his feet and use his hands more for balance. He will let go with one hand and move it to another support, or even use only one hand to balance with. At this stage he will only let go of one support when he is confident that he has firm hold of another.

Later, your baby will be able to cruise along flat surfaces such as walls and will move from one piece of furniture to another, perhaps taking a brief step in between, so that he can gradually move all round a room without actually walking unaided.

When your baby is learning to walk, it is best for him to go barefoot, as socks can make his feet slip and shoes are too constricting.

tOYS TO GROW WITH

Your baby may have outgrown those toys bought for the small baby. At this stage it might be worth investing in a few well-chosen toys which will last.

Shape-sorters and nesting boxes are reliable favorites; your baby will enjoy just looking at different shapes and manipulating them well before he can sort or stack them in an orderly way. Toys where rings or other shapes are stacked on a central pole will interest a baby in different ways as his skills develop, and building blocks and simple construction toys may keep him amused for long periods, even if he can only take them apart at this stage. Some babies enjoy simple jigsaws where they can remove the pieces with little knobs. You will have to join in with this play; you put the toy back together, and the baby takes it apart.

Toys made from household objects will also keep your baby happy: boxes to crawl in and out of, cartons which he can fill and empty with objects like corks and spools. All babies love to empty their mother's handbag, so why not take an old bag and fill it with a selection of things he can remove at will?

A baby of this age will enjoy a baby wagon which he can load with toys. Now is the time he will really need it, when he is learning to stand and walk, rather than waiting until his first birthday when he may be walking or be on the point of walking alone. Before your baby starts using such toys, check that stairs are guarded and glass doors replaced with safety glass.

Toys on strings are good at this age. Besides the simple wooden or plastic ones, there are also more interesting animals which wag their tails, shake their heads, bob up and down or make a noise as they are pulled along. Your baby may also be amused by puppets or dolls which you can operate for him.

Other favorite toys are a jack in the box (although these make some babies cry) and music boxes which they can operate themselves by pulling a string or opening a lid. Many babies love anything musical and you can buy simple instruments, such as bells.

Books are popular with all young children, especially colorful picture books with bold images and little writing. From rag books and board books he can progress to sturdy 'real' books'. You will need to turn the pages for him and name the pictures.

See Week 51 for Walking

See Week 52 for First Birthday Presents

week 46

month   *date*

MON

TUES

WED

THURS

FRI

SAT

SUN

Burns and scalds
● Immerse the area in cold (not ice) water immediately.
● Take off any tight clothes.
● Call the doctor or go straight to the hospital.
● If a child's clothes are on fire, douse them with water or smother them with a towel, blanket or coat. (Beware of using synthetic fabrics which could catch fire.)

Choking
● Call for emergency medical services.
● Hold your baby face down over your arm (or hold her by the legs and turn her upside down) and give her five sharp slaps between the shoulder blades.
● If this doesn't work, lie her in front of you and give five rapid chest thrusts over the breastbone, using two fingers. If the baby does not start to breathe immediately, place your mouth over the mouth and nose of the baby, and do two quick, shallow breaths.
● Never try to scoop out an object wedged at the back of her throat, as this could lodge it more firmly.

Poisoning
● If breathing has stopped, start CPR immediately. Call the poison control center or take her straight to the hospital, with the container if you know what it was.
● Do *not* give milk or water unless instructed by the experts at the poison-control center.
● Don't give her anything to try to make her vomit unless told to do so by experts.

Electric shock
● Switch off the source of power or break the electrical contact: use something that won't transmit electricity (like a wooden broom) to push the baby away.

If you are in any doubt about the extent of your child's injuries, call for medical help at once.

*n*OTES

SAFETY AND FIRST AID

*b*y the time your baby becomes upright and is very mobile you will have had to adapt your house to minimize the chances of an accident. If you are aware of the most common causes of accidents to children, you can do everything possible to avoid these. However, no matter how careful you are, there is always the possibility of an unforeseen happening and it is also important to know how to deal with an emergency if it arises. In rare instances you need to know how to do mouth-to-mouth resuscitation if the baby has stopped breathing, or heart compressions if her heart has stopped. You can best learn these by going on a first-aid course such as those that are provided locally by organizations like The American Red Cross and your local first aid squad.

SENSIBLE PRECAUTIONS

Burns and scalds are common serious accidents, so take sensible precautions to protect your child from these. Never put hot cups of tea and coffee within a baby's reach and always turn saucepan handles on the stove inward. Make sure all fires are either guarded or extinguished; never leave electrical equipment plugged in.

Poisoning is another hazard, so keep all poisonous substances out of reach and locked away – not only medicines but also bleach, cleaning fluids, detergents, alcoholic drinks, and perfumes. Where possible, buy substances in bottles with child-resistant lids. Keep plastic bags out of baby's reach or punch holes in them.

Small objects Don't let your baby get hold of objects which she could swallow and choke on. Ballpoint pen tops and the plastic clips used to fasten bags of bread are dangerous items which have caused child deaths.

Sharp pins and hooks are also potentially dangerous. Never leave your child unattended in the bath as a baby can drown in only a small depth of water.

Your child will have many tumbles in her first year; she will usually howl when hurt and may develop bruises but most of the time it is unlikely to be serious.

DANGER SIGNALS

If your baby bangs her head with quite a hard knock, take her to the doctor if she shows any of the following signs:

- She is unconscious, even briefly;
- She does not cry when hurt and is drowsy;
- She vomits after the accident;
- She is bleeding from the ears or nose;
- She is bleeding profusely;
- Her behavior appears abnormal to you.

week 47

month _____ date _____

MON

TUES

WED

THURS

FRI

SAT

SUN

*n*OTES

It is useful to keep a first-aid kit in the house and another in the car if you have one. You can buy ready-made first-aid kits from the pharmacy, or you can make your own. You will need adhesive bandages, gauze bandages, absorbent cotton, safety pins or surgical tape, blunt-ended tweezers, antiseptic cream or lotion, an antiseptic solution or surgical alcohol (or antiseptic wipes for convenience), calamine lotion or other soothing ointment for sunburn or stings, acetaminophen syrup, and a thermometer.

If your baby has more than a mild injury, you will need to use first-aid treatment or see a doctor. You can treat minor cuts and bruises by cleaning the wound with warm water, applying antiseptic cream and covering with a bandage or dressing. Blisters should never be popped, and are best left alone; if a blister is somewhere where it is rubbing, cover it with a bandage or dressing. If the blister bursts, keep it clean and dry.

Small objects like a speck of dirt in the eye can usually be removed by bathing the eye with absorbent cotton and warm (preferably boiled) water. Don't let your child touch it. If the object is larger or won't come out, consult a doctor.

Many small children put foreign bodies in their ears or nose. Don't try to remove an object from the ear yourself as you may wedge it in more firmly – see a doctor instead. If there is a foreign body in the nose, block one nostril and get the child to blow through the other (this is difficult with a baby). If it won't come out, again see a doctor.

Small children can easily swallow a small, round object like a marble. Usually this will go through their system without causing any harm, but any signs of pain or discomfort should be taken seriously.

*t*HE OLDER BABY'S CLOTHES

*a*s your baby gets older you will probably want to dress him or her in more individualistic clothes, but these should always be comfortable and practical. Dresses are pretty for little girls and are practical for the baby who sits or who is walking, but they are a nuisance for the crawler. If your baby girl does wear dresses, she will need warm tights to cover her diaper and keep her legs warm in winter, or she could wear bodysuits which fasten underneath to keep her tummy warm.

Jogging suits and overalls are practical and popular for children of both sexes and are likely to last longer than one-piece suits. Tight clothes will restrict your active baby's movements and you should never put on suits in which the toes are too tight, or socks that are too small, as this will restrict his growing feet. The feet of stretch suits and socks are slippery for a mobile baby; he can go barefoot or, in winter, wear soft corduroy footwear with non-slip soles which keep feet warm without restricting them. You can buy these practical shoe substitutes in various sizes; some have cords which you can tighten round the ankles and others have elastic. Check that there is plenty of room inside and that the elastic isn't too tight around the ankles. They are also very useful for outdoor wear in the winter if your baby's snow suit doesn't have toes.

For the winter, warm jackets and one-piece suits are essential, and in really cold weather it is

a good idea to have a hat that covers the ears or has ear flaps. Keep something warm on the baby's feet in winter too. If you use mittens, try tying them together with string and threading them through the arms of his coat because he will probably try to pull them off all the time.

FIRST SHOES

Do not be tempted to buy your baby's first shoes too early. It is usually best to wait until he is actually walking and you want him to walk out of doors. His feet are growing very rapidly and may change shape when he starts walking properly, as they become more arched; they may also get wider as he puts

his weight on them and the toes splay out. So shoes fitted before he is walking may not fit correctly, or may be outgrown, once he starts to walk.

Always take your baby to a shoe store to have his feet measured for his first shoes. You may find it best to invest in a good-quality leather shoe,

especially for the first pair, since they will fit more comfortably and this may be important in giving your child confidence in walking.

Check the baby's foot size frequently once he starts wearing shoes, as tight shoes will restrict growth and may even deform the foot.

week 48

month   *date*

MON

TUES

WED

THURS

FRI

SAT

SUN

*n*OTES

HEALTHY TEETH

Once your baby has several teeth, you should start to clean them after meals with a toothbrush and a small quantity of toothpaste. If you are giving fluoride supplements, beware of her swallowing much fluoride toothpaste or she may get too high a dose.

Never let your baby go to sleep sucking a bottle of milk or juice as this can damage her teeth.

Your baby's diet is also important for keeping teeth healthy. Cut out over-sweetened foods, especially in convenience meals, and don't give sweet things in between. If your baby wants a snack, try a low-salt cracker or biscuit, lump of cheese or a piece of fruit or raw vegetable.

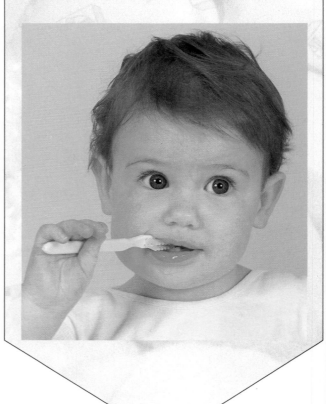

KEEPING YOUR BABY CLEAN

*a*s your baby gets older you might face problems in keeping her clean and well-cared for because she may resist all your attempts to do so. It can be a struggle to hold a wriggling baby down while you change her diaper; she may pull away and howl when you wipe her sticky face and hands; and she may refuse to keep still while you trim her nails and comb her hair. The best way is to try to make a game out of all these activities and to choose your moment so as to get least resistance.

To make diaper changing easier, keep some interesting objects nearby to entertain your baby while she's on the changing mat; give them to her to look at before you lie her down.

If she hates having her face and hands wiped, try using a warm soft cloth and tickle her with it a few times before giving her a gentle wipe. Play 'This little piggy' with her fingers as you wipe them. You can try the same technique when cutting finger- and toenails: it helps if you cut these when she's out of a warm bath, when her nails are softer. Never force her to keep still, which can turn this exercise into a battle and make her resist further. If it's really impossible to get her cooperation, try to cut your baby's nails when she is fast asleep.

Some babies develop a dislike of having their hair washed when they get older. One trick is to wet the hair gently while she's in the bath, using as little water as possible, and shampoo it with the minimum of non-stinging shampoo. If the water temperature is just right, she will hardly notice it. Then take a towel or dry wash cloth and hold it over her forehead while you swiftly rinse the hair to prevent any water and shampoo from getting on her face and in her eyes. Again, turn swooshing the water down her back into a game and make her laugh. You can get specially designed shields to protect your baby's face while washing her hair, which can make for happier bathtimes.

Your older baby will probably not mind being dressed and undressed too much and should be able to cooperate by moving her arms to get them in and out of armholes, rather than holding them stiff.

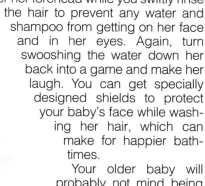

week 49

MON

TUES

WED

THURS

FRI

SAT

SUN

MESSY PLAY

Most babies love an opportunity to make a mess, though they're seldom allowed this luxury. If your baby seems bored or if you want to give him something new and exciting to do, why not set aside some time for this?

Put him in a high chair with a protective garment on and give him some paper and some finger paints. He may enjoy 'drawing' a picture with stubby wax crayons; you could sit him on your lap for this more controllable activity.

Make up some 'play dough' with flour and water and let him poke, knead and finger it to his heart's content. Again, restrain him in the high chair if you don't want it to end up all over the room. In the summer, let him play with sand and water outdoors.

A baby's attention span is very short at this age and he may be interested in one of these activities for only two or three minutes. This will seem a short time for all the preparation and mess involved, but he will gradually want to play for longer and longer periods.

notes

*Y*oung babies don't usually pay much attention to other babies of the same age. They will not really 'play' together till the age of eighteen months or more, and then quite a lot of their interaction will not be play but it will consist of fighting over toys.

Nevertheless, it's good for your baby to get used to being with other children in preparation for later on, when children really need to be sociable. It's important to teach your child to share, not just toys and games but also your attention. Minding a friend's baby for a morning can teach him that he can't always have your undivided attention. And although two babies may seem not to interact, you may notice that they play quietly together on the floor for longer than they would normally do on their own.

It is a good idea to start or join a playgroup, especially if you don't know many mothers in the area with children of the same age as yours. Joining a playgroup will provide your baby with the opportunity to explore new environments and play with new toys. You will probably find being with other mothers whose children are at roughly the same stage of development extremely helpful and reassuring, and you may make lasting friendships. The National Association for the Education of Young Children can provide information on how to set up a playgroup (see Useful Addresses, p. 110).

APPROACHING ONE-YEAR

No longer helpless, babies are on the move and 'into everything.' They're climbing on chairs, shaking tables, and literally picking up anything and everything that isn't nailed down or locked away. It's just about all any parent can do to keep up with them. But parents should really rejoice. This is exactly what babies are supposed to be doing at this age.

However, it's imperative, if you haven't already, to 'baby-proof' your house from top to bottom. Windows should have guards, stairs gates; put covers on electrical outlets, bulbs in empty lamp sockets; toilet seats and diaper pails should be covered; glass doors replaced with safety glass; guns locked up; plastic bags out of reach, etc.

week 50

MON

TUES

WED

THURS

FRI

SAT

SUN

FIRST WORDS

Your baby may produce her first words at around this time. Even if she doesn't produce anything intelligible, she will carry out long conversations with you in quite complex babble. If you sing to her, you may find that she sings along too.

It's very important to talk to your baby. She will take great pleasure in your imitating the sounds she makes and in trying to copy the sounds you make. She will also understand a great deal of what you say and you can play simple 'Where is it?' games together. Ask 'Where's mummy's nose?' and point to that. Your baby will soon catch on and may do the pointing herself.

*n*OTES

*b*y the end of the first year, your baby will probably be ready to give up breast- or bottle-feedings entirely. Whether you decide to wean her from the breast or put away the bottle at this stage depends partly on you and partly on the baby. Some mothers find that their baby gradually loses interest, so that when you sit down to breast-feed her she laughs, giggles, tries to stand up or wiggle off your lap. She may even bite. She may start to feed and then, perhaps when your milk lets down, lose interest and do something else.

A bottle-fed baby may drink less and less of her bottle, or resent having to sit still on your lap while she takes it. A baby who behaves like this is really trying to tell you that she's ready to give up, and will not miss the breast- or bottle-feedings if you stop them.

If you are ready to wean your baby from the breast or don't want her to continue having a bottle, you will probably jump at this opportunity. But some mothers enjoy breast-feeding so much that they don't want to stop yet, and others are convinced that without their bedtime bottle-feeding their baby won't go to sleep.

Some babies, on the other hand, really seem to need to suck for longer and will be happier continuing with a bedtime feeding.

Milk is a food that is a useful source of protein and vitamins throughout childhood. As long as your baby is getting milk in cooking, or in alternative sources such as cheese and yogurt, you don't have to worry about her not drinking milk as much. If your baby still drinks a lot of milk, you may find she becomes fussy at meal times because she is not really hungry. Overcome this problem by giving drinks of milk after the meal.

See Week 42 for Weaning to a Cup

BALANCED MEALS FOR AN OLDER BABY

Soups
You can make nutritious soups for your baby and the whole family. Simply cook vegetables till soft, with chicken or other stock, and use a food processor or blender to liquidize it so that nothing is lost. Try old favorites like pea and ham (use dried split peas), and carrot and orange. You can add pasta shapes to the soup or break a whole egg into it shortly before serving. You can thin it and cool it down by adding milk. Children often love to dip things in their food, so try making bread 'soldiers'.

Sandwiches
Sandwiches can provide a healthy balanced meal for your older baby. Choose wholewheat bread, butter thinly and use a variety of fillings – peanut butter (smooth, preferably without salt), cheese, boiled egg, minced roast chicken, beef or lamb, and tomatoes, cucumber (chopped) or fruit such as ripe pears. Use a cookie cutter to make interesting shapes.

Try to use bread which is not too dry or crumbly, and cut off the crusts if your baby always leaves them. Avoid '7-grain' style bread.

Alternative ideas
If your child dislikes certain foods, you can usually find alternatives she prefers. A baby who doesn't like vegetables can get most of the vitamins and fiber from fruit instead; a baby who doesn't like meat can get protein from dairy products, fish (try boneless, soft fish like flounder or cod) and eggs. Or you can try some health food products such as tofu (soya bean spread), which is very bland in taste and texture and can easily be mixed in with other foods, or seed spreads like tahini.

week 51

month	date

MON

TUES

WED

THURS

FRI

SAT

SUN

*n*OTES

WALKING

The majority of babies do not walk till after their first birthday – the average age is about thirteen months.

You can encourage your child to take a few steps by crouching down in front of him, holding out your arms and catching him when he launches himself forward. Once he has taken a step or two, move slowly a little further away. He will probably fall over a lot when he is first walking, so don't let him walk on very hard or rough surfaces where he could hurt himself and lose confidence.

*y*OU: ONE YEAR LATER

a whole year has passed since your baby was born. Now is a good time to take stock. You may find being a full-time mother very rewarding and have made lots of friends with whom to share the experience. If not, you may be finding that after a year dedicated to the baby you want to do more for yourself and perhaps take on some part-time work or a daytime or evening adult education class to develop other aspects of yourself. You may want to spend more time with your partner and create some time for the two of you to be alone.

A year after the birth you may be thinking about when is the best time to plan another baby – unless you have decided that one is enough! Mothers often wonder if there is a 'best' gap between two children in a family. The answer is probably not; there are advantages and disadvantages to each age gap. Any gap under eighteen months is likely to be physically very hard on the mother but would enable her to go back to work once her family is complete, without being at home for too many years.

A short gap may mean that there is almost no break between the end of breast-feeding and the start of another pregnancy, so the drain on your body is considerable. A close gap also means two babies in diapers at the same time, that you may be dealing with potty training as well as constantly feeding a small baby. On the other hand, the elder child may be too young to express much jealousy and will soon adjust to the new baby because he can't remember that life was any different. When the children grow older they will be closer developmentally and may play very well together for that reason.

A larger gap is likely to be less exhausting for the mother; there will be a period in which to recover physically and emotionally from the first baby before entering the second pregnancy. If the elder child is at playgroup or nursery school there will be more time for you to give to each child individually. However, older children may be more jealous of a baby as they understand more what is going on and can remember what life was like before they had to share their parents' love. Later on, if their interests and skills are very different, they may be less good playmates and fight some of the time. However, the second child often acquires skills at an earlier age, especially if helped by an older brother or sister, and the two can have fun together.

Some mothers feel that now is the time to plan a second baby so that the two children are close in age. Others feel they cannot contemplate another child for some time yet.

week 52

month   date

MON

_____

TUES

_____

WED

_____

THURS

_____

FRI

_____

SAT

_____

SUN

_____

NOTES

FIRST BIRTHDAY PRESENTS

Friends and relatives will probably buy presents for your baby and may consult you on what she would like. Give some thought to this, as you may have bought some toys and may prefer toys that your baby will grow into around eighteen months.

A ride-on toy, such as a simple tricycle (without pedals) or a car which the child propels with her legs, will start to be fun soon after the age of one. She will get a lot of pleasure from a traditional jointed teddy bear now so this is a good idea for a present. From around twelve months children start to get real enjoyment out of books. Pop-up books and activity books of different kinds provide novel entertainment, and she will continue to love picture books with bold illustrations.

A blackboard and easel will come in at some time during the second year, and can be adapted for a variety of different uses. For the summer months, a wading pool or sandpit make good outdoor play equipment.

Don't forget Your baby will need a TB test now and a measles, mumps and rubella vaccination and booster HIB at fifteen months.

_y_our baby's first birthday is a very special occasion and it is worth giving some thought to how you would like to celebrate it. Your baby is unlikely to know what is going on herself, so plan how you think she would like to spend the day, and decide what you and your partner can do to make it special.

Other babies of this age are unlikely to interact much so a children's party, as such, is not really appropriate. However, you could ask other mothers and babies for tea and a special cake – perhaps something simple and nutritious like the carrot cake recipe (below).

You may decide that a family get-together is the most suitable form of celebration, with you and grandparents and perhaps other close family members or friends whom you and your baby know well.

You may like to spend a quiet evening with your partner thinking about the events of a year ago and looking at photographs, recalling details of the birth and how you felt about it. In the everyday hurly-burly of looking after your child, it is easy to lose sight of how miraculous her birth was.

See Week 45 for Toys to Grow With

To help your baby enjoy a first birthday, wrap presents in lots of paper, babies love tearing wrappers off presents. Balloons are another great favorite – but be careful because babies can choke on them, too. Blowing out the candle may not be so easy to do!

PARTY CARROT CAKE

1 cup flour (wholewheat if preferred)
2 tsp baking powder
1/2 cup finely grated carrot
4 oz butter
1/2 cup brown sugar
grated rind of a lemon or orange
2 eggs, lightly beaten
2 tbs milk
Cream together butter and sugar, then add rind and eggs and beat till smooth. Add carrot, then gradually add flour and baking powder and use milk if required to make a soft mixture.

Grease a cake pan and fill it with the mixture. Bake in a preheated oven (325°F) for about 30 minutes, or until the cake is done and golden brown in colour.

Cheese topping:
6oz cream cheese
4oz confectioner's sugar
Mix the cream cheese and confectioner's sugar together and use to fill the cake and cover the top. Decorate with pieces of fruit such as tangerine slices. Make a face or picture on the cake with fruit or other decorations.

USEFUL ADDRESSES

POSTNATAL SUPPORT

Depression After Delivery
P.O. Box 1282
Morrisville, PA 19067
800-944-4773 (toll-free)
Clearinghouse for emotional support
through volunteer contacts throughout the
US.

La Leche League International
P.O. Box 4079
Schaumburg, IL 60168-4079
708-519-7730
Breastfeeding information and support
(check phone directory for local chapter
or write to above address).

**National Organization of Mothers of Twins
Clubs Inc.**
P.O. Box 23188
Albuquerque, NM 87192-1188
505-275-0955
Complimentary informational brochure and
referral to nearest support group.

**National Sudden Infant Death Syndrome
Foundation**
1314 Bedford Avenue
Suite 210, Baltimore, MD 21208
410-653-8226
800-221-SIDS (toll-free)
Information and referrals to local chapters.

Parents for Prematures
13613 NW 26th Place
Bellevue, WA 98005
Support for parents of premature babies.

Postpartum Support International
c/o Jane Honikman
927 N. Kellogg Ave.
Santa Barbara, CA 93111
805-967-7636
International network for support groups
and professionals concerned with
depression after delivery issues.

SUPPORT AND
INFORMATION FOR
PARENTS

**American Association for Marriage and
Family Therapy**
1100 17th St., N.W.
Washington, DC 20006
202-452-0109
Provides lists of division presidents in your
area.

**American Speech-Language-Hearing
Association**
10801 Rockville Pike
Rockville, MD 20852
800-678-8255 (toll-free helpline, voice and

TDD.)
Information on communicative disorders
in children.

AuPair Homestay USA
1522 K Street, N.W.
Suite 1100
Washington, D.C. 20003
202-628-7134

AuPair in America
100 Greenwich Avenue
Greenwich, CT 06830
203-869-9090

Childhelp U.S.A.
6463 Independence Ave.
Woodland Hills, CA 91367
800-4-A-CHILD (24-Hour hotline for victims
of child abuse, parents who think they
might abuse their children, and anyone
reporting suspected child abuse.)

Children in Hospitals, Inc.
31 Wilshire Park
Needham, MA 02192
617-482-2915
Offers help and advice on negotiating with
hospital staff in order to minimize the
trauma of hospitalization.

**National Association of Childcare
Resources and Referral Agencies
(NACCRA)**
2116 Campus Drive S.E.
Rochester, MN 55904
507-287-2020

**National Association for the Education of
Young Children**
1509 16th St., NW
Washington, DC 20036
Information about early education, birth–8.

National Association of Mothers' Centers
336 Fulton Ave.
Hempstead, NY 11550
516-486-6614
800-645-3828 (toll free)
Help in locating mothers' centers near you
and/or information on how to start one.

MELD (Minnesota Early Learning Design)
123 North Third Street
Minneapolis, MN 55401
(612) 332-7563
Assists parents in starting parent support
groups under auspices of local institutions.

Parents Anonymous
6733 South Sepulveda Blvd.
Suite 270
Los Angeles, CA 90045
Counseling for parents who have or who
are tempted to abuse their children.
(Check phone directory for local chapter or
write to above address.)

The Family Resource Coalition
Department P
230 North Michigan Avenue
Room 1625
Chicago, IL 60601
(312) 726-4750
Information about local parent support
groups.

United Way of America
701 N. Fairfax
Alexandria, VA 22314
703-836-7100
Provides information and referrals to health
and human care agencies; check phone
directory for local office.

INFORMATION ON
HEALTH, SAFETY AND
FIRST AID

American Academy of Pediatrics
141 Northwest Point Blvd.
P.O. Box 927
Elk Grove Village, IL 60007
800-421-0589 (toll-free, IL only)
800-433-9016 (toll-free)
Information and referrals.

Center for Science in the Public Interest
1875 Connecticut Ave., N.W.
Suite 300
Washington, D.C. 20009-5728
202-332-9110
Information on safe nutrition and advocacy.

**National Child Passenger Safety
Association**
Suite 300
1707 DeSales Street
Washington, D.C. 20036
202-429-0515
Answers questions on automobile safety.

**National Highway Traffic Safety
Administration**
400 Seventh Street S.W.
Washington, D.C. 20590
800-424-9393 (auto safety hotline)
202-426-0123 (in Washington, D.C. only)

National Safety Council
444 N. Michigan Ave.
Chicago, IL 60611
312-527-4800
800-621-7619 (toll-free)
Information on safe toys and furniture,
safety restraints, etc.

U.S. Consumer Product Safety Commission
1750 K St., N.W.
Washington, D.C. 20207
800-638-2772 (toll-free for information on
recalls on children's toys and furniture;
complaints about unsafe children's items.).

When writing for information please enclose
a stamped addressed envelope.

*i*NDEX

*a*CKNOWLEDGMENTS

Conran Octopus wish to thank the following for their help in the preparation of this book:

For advising on the text: Ros Meek, Assistant Public Relations Officer, Health Visitors' Association.

For taking part in the photography: Edward and Jeremy Hamand, Leonora Russell, Louise and Francesca Taylor, Gerry and Katherine Kensley.

For jacket photographs: Dale Durfee (front jacket); Susanna Price/Bubbles (back jacket).

For their permission to reproduce photographs: 1 Tony Stone Picture Library/Paul Harrison; **2** Clement/Jerrican; **4** Loisjoy Thurston/Bubbles; **7** Crampon/Jerrican; **8** Anthea Sieveking/Vision International; **9** © 1992 Comstock/Sandra Lousada SGC; **14** Loisjoy Thurston/Bubbles; **16** Sally & Richard Greenhill; **18** Sandra Lousada/Susan Griggs Agency; **19** Reflections Photo Library/Jennie Woodcock; **21** Susanna Price/Bubbles; **23** Mothercare UK Limited; **24** Zefa Picture Library; **27** Pierre Hinous/Agence Top; **28** Valerie Clement/Jerrican; **29** Tony Stone Picture Library/David Sutherland; **31** Loisjoy Thurston/Bubbles; **33** © 1992 Comstock/Sandra Lousada SGC; **35** Reflections Photo Library/Jennie Woodcock; **37** © 1992 Comstock/Sandra Lousada SGC; **39** Loisjoy Thurston/Bubbles; **41** Pictor International; **42** Jennie Woodcock; **43** Loisjoy Thurston/Bubbles; **45** Schuster/Robert Harding Picture Library; **46** Loisjoy Thurston/Bubbles; **47** Loisjoy Thurston/Bubbles; **49** J.M. Trois/Explorer; **53** Reflections Photo Library/Jennie Woodcock; **54** Pictor International; **56** © 1992 Comstock/Sandra Lousada SGC; **57** © 1992 Comstock/Sandra Lousada SGC; **58** Richard Yard/Bubbles; **61** Tony Evans/Robert Harding Picture Library; **65** © 1992 Comstock/Sandra Lousada SGC; **66** Jeremy Hamand; **67** Mothercare UK Limited; **69** Hutchison Picture Library; **71** Sandra Lousada/Conran Octopus; **73** Lupe Cunha; **75** above Mothercare UK Limited; **75** below Delimage/Explorer; **77** Jacqui Farrow/Bubbles; **78** © 1992 Comstock/Sandra Lousada SGC; **81** J.F. Besnard/Agence Top; **83** Reflections Photo Library/Jennie Woodcock; **84** Loisjoy Thurston/Bubbles; **85** Susanna Price/Bubbles; **86** Tony Stone Picture Library/Andy Cox; **87** Reflections Photo Library/Jennie Woodcock; **89** Reflections Photo Library/Jennie Woodcock; **90** Loisjoy Thurston/Bubbles; **93** © 1992 Comstock/Sandra Lousada SGC; **95** Anthea Sieveking/Collections; **97** Ian West/Bubbles; **99** Camera Press; **100** Loisjoy Thurston/Bubbles; **101** Tony Stone Picture Library/Andy Cox; **103** Reflections Photo Library/Jennie Woodcock; **106** Labout/Jerrican; **107** Tony Stone Picture Library/Andy Cox; **109** Lupe Cunha.